Praise for Pathworking with the Egyptian Gods

This tenderly crafted book takes you to the core of the mystery that was ancient Egypt. A mystery that cannot be accessed with your head, only with your heart and with your senses so beautifully evoked by this intimate guide. To explore in the hands of such experienced pathworkers is a wonderous gift. Treasure it.

Judy Hall, author of *The Crystal Bible* and *Torn Clouds*

GW00385529

PATHWORKING
WITH THE
EGYPTIAN
GODS

Judith Page is a well known artist specializing in representations of Egyptian pantheon groups with a strong emphasis on astronomy. Her work has been featured in numerous magazines and books.

Jan A. Malique (United Kingdom) is a scholar and writer whose life-long passion is ancient Egypt. For over twenty-five years, she has also practiced healing methods, magic, and mysticism.

Judith Page
Jan A. Malique

Foreword by Alan Richardson

PATHWORKING

WITH THE

EGYPTIAN

GODS

Llewellyn Publications
Woodbury, Minnesota

First Edition
First Printing, 2010

Cover art: Parchment © Winston Davidian, illustration © Dave Stevenson / Jennifer
    Vaughn Artist Agent
Cover design by Lisa Novak
Editing by Patti Frazee
Interior illustrations by Llewellyn art department

Llewellyn is a registered trademark of Llewellyn Worldwide Ltd.

Library of Congress Cataloging-in-Publication Data
Page, Judith, 1960–
  Pathworking with the Egyptian gods / Judith Page, Jan A. Malique ;
foreword by Alan Richardson. — 1st ed.
     p.   cm.
  ISBN 978-0-7387-1906-1
  1. Magic. 2. Gods, Egyptian. 3. Meditations. I. Malique, Jan A.,
1963– II. Title.
  BF1623.G63P35 2010
  299'.31—dc22

                                                           2010014352

Llewellyn Publications
A Division of Llewellyn Worldwide Ltd.
2143 Wooddale Drive
Woodbury, MN 55125-2989
www.llewellyn.com

Printed in the United States of America

OTHER BOOKS BY JUDITH PAGE

The Song of Set

Song of Meri-Khem

Theft of the 7 Ankhs

This book is dedicated to the late Elizabeth St. George, author, who was our initiator, mentor, and guiding light in the darkness. Spiritually, she guided our feet and helped us recognize, and act upon, every choice we must make in order that we see the signs leading to where the powerful forces of the original creator intended for us, and in doing so, serve him perfectly as we were created to do. Through her we found the Pathways to the Neters.

ACKNOWLEDGMENTS

I thank my co-author and best friend Jan for helping tackle a most difficult and serious piece of work. Her material added that extra quality of magick and beauty.

I thank too my partner Alain Leroy for helping with the research for the epigraphs of the Egyptian gods. Stephen Quirke, B.A., Ph.D., Professor in Egyptology, Curator of the Petrie Museum, for checking and advising on the hieroglyphs used throughout the book. Alan Richardson, friend and fellow accomplice in the arts magickal, for always being there when I needed a sounding board regarding my work, and Judy Hall for not just giving her appraisal on *Pathworking with the Egyptian Gods*, but her comfort and support at a time when I was very low. She helped get me through an extremely difficult time in my life. A special thanks to Maxine Sanders, who taught me the art of visualisation; without this important ingredient, there would be no magick.

—Judith Page

All love and thanks to the guiding force behind Ptah. May this work be a suitable offering, Great One. I thank my partner David Almond for his considerable support and encouragement, especially where this book was concerned. I also thank my co-author and friend Judith for believing in me and giving me the opportunity to put down on paper words of devotion to the Neters that were locked in my heart. Last but not least, humble thanks to Anpu for initiating a journey many, many years ago which has reunited me with trusted teachers and companions of the magickal arts.

—Jan Malique

CONTENTS

FOREWORD

The plain fact is, most of the pathworkings that are published these days are just short stories written by those who have neither real knowledge nor vital experience, and who substitute purple prose for magickal insight, hoping that no one will notice. With rare exceptions they are sorry and literally spiritless tomes that blight the bookshelves in increasing numbers.

Pathworking with the Egyptian Gods, however, could not be further removed from this genre, and is clearly the work of many lifetimes. Judith Page and Jan Malique have created a powerful and practical book in which you can approach the major deities of ancient Egypt on differing levels: practical, intellectual, emotional, and spiritual. The evocations are unusual, and even on the first reading you are left in no doubt that these two women really have trod those paths, and made contact with the gods and goddesses of Egypt. These are not mere pictures in the head that they describe, but eternal energies, ever-becoming. The analyses of such figures as Osiris and Set are unexpected, forcing you to revise old opinions, thereby reenergising these archetypes in your own psyche.

Be warned: this book will give you powerful, beautiful, and occasionally disturbing dreams—disturbing because you will wake in the morning with the thought: *that was real*. It will take you beyond time and into the heart of ancient Egypt in a way that physical travel never could.

Alan Richardson
Wiltshire, England, 2008

INTRODUCTION

The art of pathworking even for the beginner takes no time to master, and almost everyone has a result right from the beginning. Pathworking is one of the most powerful magickal tools we have for aligning ourselves with the energies of the deities, and travelling to the inner worlds of the ancient gods, which are real, and so too are the changes that occur there.

Not only will this book be an aid to the advanced practitioner, but it will also be a valuable learning tool for those who are just beginning to practise pathworking.

True, there are so many books on ancient Egypt, initiation, and magick that the reader is spoilt for choice. This book not only combines all three, but also brings the reader in touch with the ancient gods of Egypt by means of a path to meet, learn, and work with them.

The way, or pattern, of thinking of an ancient Egyptian may appear to be lost to us on the physical plane, but it still lives within the names of her gods, her ruined temples, the scorching heat of the sun, and in the whisper of the wind as it weaves its way through the land. We just need to still our minds and hearts in order to reach out and embrace this hidden world. This we shall do by undertaking a journey to the sacred centres along the Nile and commune with the Neters, heart to heart, and mind to mind.

Pathworking will help you understand yourself, gain an insight into your nature, and enable you to go on spiritual journeys. This method will be used as a means to discover your true inner being and also to help heal painful experiences that are locked within. You can achieve this if you are willing to let go of the past and move forward to a more positive future. As the serpent sloughs off its skin layer by layer, so shall you, the seeker and initiate, take the same path of regeneration.

You can also look upon this book as an initiatory experience, such as the one explained in *The Pilgrimage* by Paulo Coelho, that will open in the seeker a genuine and true dimension of what a real quest and initiation is all about.

With each pathworking, you unfold the quest within, since you are both the quest and the path. Whether you are an advanced student or a beginner, the goal of initiatory pathworking is the direct awakening of your consciousness to a higher level. It will involve change, perhaps welcome, perhaps not, but transmutation of stagnant and outworn energies will occur within the crucible of your soul. It will also reveal to you an awakening into a new world through the eyes of an older one. You can look upon the Neters as master—"When the disciple is ready, the master appears"—so strange encounters and inexplicable events that take place in the pathworkings may alter your states of awareness and open a way of self-initiation. It can happen suddenly, awakening your very soul to your true self. You *will* become the alchemist seeking the Philosopher's Stone, seeing all in front of you with clarity and an honesty, but ever mindful of the Great Work. Are you prepared to surrender yourself to this process?

There are several forms of pathworking, known as active and passive. Active engages the mental power and tends to be directed. This is the most common magickal technique taught in occult schools, as it takes control of the thought processes by using a set of intellectually understood symbols and active contemplation that guides the pathworker along a specific thought process toward a realisation, or a spiritual goal.

The pathworking known as passive is where the images are allowed to rise at will once the mind has been focussed on the opening symbol.

Some symbols and images can get very complicated and are not always as they seem. Unless you are completely familiar with them, they may prove confusing. This type of pathworking is of more use to an advanced student of the magickal arts, as a beginner is likely to go off on tangents and can get very easily lost in strange or bizarre associations that may prove tricky to extract oneself from.

A note for beginners: if this should occur, just push away the association you recognise as taking you away from your goal, stay calm, and refocus, and this should get you back on track.

All pathworkings have a beginning, a middle, and an end. Your journeys will always begin in front of two great pylons, forming a gate through which you can leave your world behind, and by which you can return. These pylons should be built with love and care. You will recognize each stone and marking on them. Think of the great pylons at the entrance of Karnak Temple as you build yours. Visualise the pale gold of the sandstone and smell the warmth of the sunlight as it falls on it.

Imagine feeling the coolness as you pass through the portal and into a landscape that will take you into the heart of ancient Khemit. You will learn how to focus on its energy as you are drawn in. This is the type of structure you will envisage each time you go on your journey. Your pylons will be your safeguard.

You will end your journey much as you began it. You will return to the mundane world through the pylons, hearing the gates close behind you. It is important to hear those gates closing, so click your fingers and stamp your feet. Many problems can erupt if the gates are not properly closed. It is just common sense and makes for good psychic hygiene. Doorways have been opened both mentally and astrally, and you need to ensure nothing comes through which is going to negatively affect either you or your environment.

Not only will you be going on a pathworking, but a journey into the soul of the many temples. Each one will give you insight into a god or goddess who will impart to you the secrets and mysteries that lie within the culture of this ancient land. You will learn to merge in with the environment and also to interact with the main players, the Neters. They are real and potent energies, stripped bare of millennia of our projected desires, hopes, and misconceptions. Approach them with respect and you will find the way opens up before you. Some Neters you may come to love with all your heart.

We have chosen Djehuty to be your guide; most of you will know him as Thoth. He will accompany you as you embark on your pathworkings throughout Khemit. Djehuty was not only the god of writing and knowledge, but was believed in ancient times to have been a "time lord." He symbolises many things: balance, truthfulness, complete knowledge, and wisdom and, being "Lord of the Holy Words," he held the power to create and destroy. With him, you, the seeker, will find many doors being opened and much that is hidden brought to light. All that is asked of you is that you are honest and sincere in your efforts to seek knowledge of your self and the Universe.

As you work with the individual Neter during your pathworking, you will be mindful of ritual elements, blessings, consecrations, hymns, and, most important of all, the Neter's name. As Kagemni, the Sixth Dynasty philosopher, wrote: "He holds fast to the Neter's name and inspires others to meditate on it."

In addition to the common name of any god, like Heru for Horus, they also had a hidden name, a name of power that the priests and priestesses used in ritual and meditation. In your first working, *Path to Isis,* your personal magickal name will be revealed to you, which you will use through all your pathworkings. It will be known only to you and the Neters and should not be revealed to anyone else. It is said that certain secrets revealed soon lose their power.

At times you may be aware of others being with you as they too travel through the ancient land of Khemit. They may appear as shadows, or shades, and you may even hear them whispering within the temple precincts. If this disturbs you, then build your pylons and leave through the portal back to your realm. You can always return when you feel the time is right. If, on the other hand, you are interrupted, visualize your temple pylon and step back through the portal to your physical level, remembering always to seal it after you.

Like names, words also had great power, especially in the ancient language of Egypt. This should not be dismissed lightly. Scientists today have discovered that sounds have power in their own right, and when vibrated at the right frequency, they can either change or destroy matter. The "Word" embodies potent power.

As you explore these temples and sacred places in your pathworking, you will be aware of passing into a different field of energy. The architects of ancient Egypt were not just designing a structure to house a god; they were actually building on a physical power zone. Each zone not only absorbed a special current of vital energy from the physical environment, but also from higher levels of cosmic consciousness. The phenomenon known as time operated in a uniquely different way within these temples.

You may be familiar with the phrase "as above, so below." To the ancient Egyptians, they were building heaven on earth.

The temple being built over the power spot would amass the magick working in it for hundreds of years. The power from that spot would seep into the temple walls and would be self-perpetuating, kept alive by devotion and ritual. The Egyptian temple was likened to a machine for maintaining and developing divine energy.

You may ask what happens when a temple is pulled down or moved to another place. That power would still be there. Remember that the ancient Egyptians would sometimes take an older temple apart and incorporate the stones into the walls and foundations of another one far away. This would be a way of getting stones already imbued with power to "pre-charge" the new temple.

The temple sites you will visit are not necessarily in any chronological order, but follow the River Nile, or Hapy, which is not only the life source of Egypt but likened to the organs of the human body (and the glands which govern the working of such organs).

You will need a map, and a simple route along the River Nile, beginning our pathworking in Aswan, then on to Kom Ombos, Edfu, Luxor, Naqada, Denderah, Abydos, Khemenu, Fayoum, Memphis, Giza (known as Rostau), and finally to Bubastis.

Whilst exploring these places, you will be aware that you are in the realm of the patron Neter. Each Neter will offer their side of the divine pattern of the creation of the ancient land of Khemit, but you are not in a position to judge them. Their role is to teach you. Some will be symbolic and, in another temple, the approach will be purely abstract.

For example, in your pathworking to Naqada you will be thrilled and elevated to the stellar heights as you witness the birth of Nut's first child Set; then another will take you to the awe-inspiring monument of Karnak in Luxor, ancient Waset the city of cities, a place of sunlight and shadow.

This pathworking is to the innermost depths of this great temple of hidden stairways and underground caverns where you will be plunged into the darker side to meet the elemental forces beneath the Temple of Khonsu and the Opet Chapel of ancient initiation.

Another pathworking is an even more symbolic journey as you tread the age-worn paving slabs of the Temple of Luxor, Ipet-resyt, embodying the true cosmic form of the star gods and the divine plan for man's mortal form.

It is the aim of this book to cut through so much of what we now think of as ancient Egypt. Although symbolic temples dedicated to Osiris and Amun will be visited, they will not be elevated as favoured centres of apparent importance or popularity. No, they will be treated equally along with all those other power zones of Khemit. So this is not a book for those who wish to pay homage to just one Neter; it will be an experience for all those who wish to embrace the origin and notion of all the ancient Neters. It is therefore best to keep an open mind when seeking connection with Old Ones, for they will present themselves as they are and not as what *we* think they are.

The worship of the star gods, such as Nut and Set, and the lunar gods, such as Djehuty and Khonsu, along with their liturgies and images, seeps through into the religions of the solar gods the old ways always remain in Egypt. In this regard, they act as the backdrop against which the Osiris and Amunite pantheon group developed.

Pathworking with the Neters is also intended to act as a guidebook on more than one level. It is our intent to return the backdrop to its original primacy, to reveal what came before Osiris, to provide an inner pathworking guide to the ancient Neters.

AUTHORS' NOTE

Egypt calls—even across the space of the world;
and across the space of the world he who knows it
is ready to come, obedient to its summons, because in thrall
to the eternal fascination of the 'land of sand, and ruins, and gold';
the land of the charmed serpent, the land of the afterglow, that may
fade away from the sky above the mountains of Libya, but that
fades never from the memory of one who has seen it from
the base of some great column, or the top of some mighty pylon;
the land that has a spell—wonderful, beautiful Egypt.

ROBERT HICHENS

The gods have been relegated to the shadows for such a long time that now is the right moment to open the gateways and let them have their rightful place in this time and era. We have both scanned the temples in Egypt and felt the pulse moving through the walls. Messages were being sent to our innermost psyche that enabled us to tune in. But we had to wait a long time to do so, as we had to develop more in our understanding of the Pharaonic mind. This book is only the tip of the pyramid, as so much more has yet to surface. Each and every reader will contribute to the ever-rippling waters that will only serve as a foundation for others to build upon.

It certainly wasn't easy assigning particular aromas to each Neter as, like humans, they all have an aroma that is unique to them, but unlike humans their aroma is hundreds of times more potent. As we are all aware, scent has a particularly powerful effect upon the brain and consciousness, human brains being no exception. Indeed, certain substances have carried the human mind over the threshold of this reality and into other realities for millennia. We are not talking about mind-altering drugs but of precious oils, unguents, and resins that have been and still are used in religious and magickal practices.

With regard to the Neters, their divine presence not only brings with it a compelling and sensual olfactory experience, but also an energetic imprint of the Universal Mind. What is experienced with each of the Neters is an energetic being who is composed of molecules of light, intermingled with molecules of the particular perfume or oil we have assigned to them, and the colour spectrum as well.

Each aroma and colour carries with it a weight of symbolism that has been reinforced over a great period of time. These are the specific keys that are being utilised to open specific doors within the consciousness of the pilgrim. Through research and regular use of such techniques, the pilgrim will be able to access the energetic field of the Neter they wish to commune with.

PRACTICAL MATTERS

There is, however, a practical side of pathworking. Consider the business of your own space and time. Most of us do not have much of either. Few of us have spare rooms where we can isolate ourselves for meditation or pathworking. Assess your situation and fit your activities as practicably as you can around your everyday life. Try to keep to a realistic schedule and adhere to it; it will help build discipline. Above all, many of us have to be discreet in our activities; we may live in freer times but the spectre of religious intolerance is still an issue to contend with. People fear what they do not understand, so be sensible and do not make life difficult for yourself. You will learn over time to cultivate the qualities of discretion and discrimination, knowing when to open up and when to keep silent. It is as much about training the mind and the body as it is about learning the practical skills of magickal work.

NOTE

Experienced practitioners may wish to skip this section and start working through the pathworkings. As for the beginner, what might you do in preparation?

- Consider your motives for deciding to read this book. What do you wish to gain from it? How will you use the knowledge contained within it? Once that is clear in your mind, you have a foundation to build the Temple of the Self upon. Our spiritual journey can start in the most mundane of ways!

- Research the history of ancient Egypt—its people, culture, society, and religion. Try to gain an understanding of the civilization and people that gave birth to such wisdom. Look at the truth with clear sight and not through "rose-tinted glasses." Use such knowledge to make informed choices. If, after reading this book, you wish to seriously undertake supervised training in a mystery school, there are many available, but be thorough in your investigations of such organizations, for the genuine ones will be quite thorough in their assessment of you. On the other hand, you may choose to work alone; again, that is no problem. Be comfortable with whatever choice you make.

- Changes will inevitably occur when the inner levels are contacted. Issues that have lain buried deep within your subconscious will begin to stir and make forays into your conscious mind. Your emotions will be stirred, in ways not to your liking, but as in any situation in life, we have to face them. Self-honesty is a difficult thing, as is self-acceptance, warts and all. A well-balanced, healthy inner state of being can equip you with the skills you need to cope with all that life can throw at you. Above all, be gentle with yourself and do not set unrealistic goals.

What might you need? We suggest you wear a plain white robe made from natural material such as cotton or linen. You can either choose to buy it or make it yourself. But, it must be your robe and no one else may be allowed to wear it. You wear that robe for pathworking, nothing else. Putting on that robe symbolizes that you are putting aside the mundane world and stepping into the world of the spirit. The Internet is a good resource to use in search of further information. For example, Servants of the Light Mystery School (S.O.L.) has information on its website regarding the making of robes and cloaks (www.servantsofthelight.org).

As you will be working with numerous different Neters, we suggest you wear a coloured sash or cord corresponding to a particular Neter (see list on page 16). A visit to your local department store may be useful; they can be a good source of materials for your magickal wardrobe.

Your local library or bookstore are other places you can visit in search of inspiration; take a look at illustrations of temple scenes depicted on the many Egyptian monuments.

ALTAR

You may want a clear surface that functions as your altar. This can range from a small table to a lockable box (in which you can store your robe and other ritual equipment). The piece of furniture used as the altar needs to be cleansed first by wiping it thoroughly with a solution of salt and water; make sure it is dried properly afterwards. You will need a couple of candlesticks, a supply of candles, and a cloth that serves as an altar cloth. You might want an incense burner.

An ancient Egyptian priest would have used an incense "spoon." The deep bowl would have held charcoal and incense. The priest would have picked up the spoon and raised it to the nose of a statue. He then would have announced that prayers and incense had reached the god.

As charcoal gets very hot and stays that way for a long time, a metal bowl containing charcoal can char a table, and a glass bowl will crack with the heat. We therefore suggest one made of earthenware. To keep the base of the bowl cool, place a layer of sand about one inch thick in the bottom of the receptacle, then the prepared charcoal on the sand. For further protection of surfaces, make sure the incense burner is placed on an insulated or fireproof mat.

Remember that very little incense goes a long way. Think of a small salt spoon. One salt spoon full of incense may be sufficient for your pathworking, especially in a small room. Working in a fog of incense smoke is not recommended, as it will penetrate a house or apartment. Some people cannot tolerate this type of smoke so you may want to consider using an oil vaporizer instead. These can be purchased from most shops. You will need a packet of tealights, which can be purchased from a supermarket. The candle goes under the bowl that contains water followed by a few drops of scented oil. This will perfume a room without smoke to worry other people. It is also less of a health and fire risk.

THE DEITY

You might want a statuette or picture of the Neter with whom you are seeking contact. There are statuettes of many Egyptian gods and goddesses about, but buying all of them would be a costly business. Be practical and realistic in your expectations, and if your budget is constrained, a picture of the Neter can serve as a focus for your worship just as well. In fact, the deity is present regardless of whether it is in the form of an illustration or an actual statuette. Remember, it is the sincerity of your feelings, not the depth of your wallet, that is important here.

Many people think that life in Egyptian temples was placid and tranquil but this is a vision seen through rose-tinted spectacles. The priests ran orphanages and schools. They ran the medical service via herb gardens. They ran festivals. They ran the death and burial services. White robes had to be laundered. Young priests had to be rehearsed, even if they were pulled from their sleeping mats at three in the morning. Older priests would need feeding after long vigils. Those who worked with the Neters were kept very busy indeed.

MEDITATION

Don't be afraid of rehearsing. Meditation does not come easily to many people. The greatest magickians and high priests have all had to start at the beginning. The great magickians have all had to practise before they became legendary figures. They all trained and sweated. They all worked to achieve magnificent results. Be realistic about your goals, pace yourself, and learn to "see" from different viewpoints, for truth can be multilayered. Remember not to lose your sense of humour amidst the "hurly-burly" of magickal activity. The gods may see fit to trip you up to deflate your ego now and again!

How often should a pathworking be done? No two pathworkers are alike in their approach to this practise, so some method of monitoring is suggested. A diary will also be a valuable record of the development of your magickal personality, as over time you are able to chart your progress, amend working methods, and discard those that do not work. For beginners, one working per week is sufficient. Invocation is not designed to take over your life, and as with everything else, should be done in moderation. The invocations will impact upon your inner and outer worlds, profoundly in the case of certain deities, so cultivate patience. A seedling tended with care, love, and patience soon develops into a strong and healthy plant, just like the developing divine consciousness.

We have taken a brief look at the practical side of pathworking. Now let us consider the more spiritual side of working with the Neters of Egypt as we begin our pathworking.

Table of Colour Cords and Aromas

Neter(s)	Colour	Aroma
White Isis	red	lotus, rose & orange blossom
Black Isis	same	cinnamon, myrrh & amber
Sobek and Harwer	purple & yellow	lotus, frankincense & amber
Horus the Elder	yellow	patchouli, pine, jasmine, musk & vanilla
Sekhmet	red & yellow	heliotrope
Nun	blue	none
Khonsu	blue & black	patchouli, gardenia & cinnamon
Amun	blue	jasmine, lavender & pine
Anpu	brown & black	sandalwood & frankincense
Meretseger	brown & red	honey, clove & cinnamon
Set the youth	black & red	cinnamon, sandalwood, amber & lemon
Hathor	yellow	jasmine, musk, vanilla & patchouli
Nut	blue & white	frankincense, myrrh, cypress & jasmine
Set	black & red	The air is heavy with sweet aromas like water drenching sun-hot sandstone, freshly cut hay in grasslands, sandstorms of the annual Khamsin after rain…
Osiris	black & green	honey, jasmine & lotus
Sobek	purple	violet
Ptah	blue & purple	carnation, frankincense & myrrh
Djehuty	blue	camphor, myrrh, violet & musk
Tefnut and Shu	blue & white	wisteria, camphor & peppermint
Set and Horus	yellow, black & red	frankincense & myrrh
Bastet	purple & white	jasmine & lavender

ONE

LEGEND OF ISIS
"Mistress of Magick"

Auset will embrace you in peace,
She will drive away the opponent from your path.
Place your face to the West
That you may illumine the Two Lands with electrum.

BOOK OF GOING FORTH BY DAY

This pathworking will bring you close to both aspects of the goddess Isis, the white and the black. As all things in life have a positive and negative polarity, so too does the feminine image of Isis. To achieve any balance in our lives, we have to be willing to accept both light and dark aspects of the Divine Feminine and remember not to sentimentalise her.

Isis is the very symbol for the feminine aspect in us all, which also applies to men. Within our souls are the dark and light sides, which reflect our emotions of love, fear, and hate. Isis is therefore portrayed as having dual aspects of light, as the mother goddess of love, and also the dark aspects that link her with magick, cunning, and illusion, most of which she learned from the god Djehuty, or Thoth.

When her husband-brother Osiris lost his manhood, she knew that she would have to work her magick in order to conceive a child. But there was a certain amount of stealth involved. She, with her sister Nephthys, took gold from the mine in Ombos, her brother Set's domain in Naqada. With this gold, Isis fashioned a phallus and attached it to Osiris's mummified form. Her magick, cunning, and illusion worked and she bore the child Horus.

However, her origins are uncertain and are believed to have come from the Nile Delta. But unlike other Egyptian deities, she did not have a centralised cult at any point throughout her worship.

The first mention of Isis date back to the Fifth Dynasty of Egypt, which is when the first literary inscriptions were found, but her following only became prominent in the latter part of Egyptian history when it began to absorb the cults of many other goddesses.

According to the Heliopitan doctrine, she was the daughter of Nut, the overarching sky, and the earth god Geb, and sister to Osiris, Haroeris (or Harwer, commonly known as Horus the Elder), Set, and Nephthys. These godlings were born in the Nile swamps on the first day between the first years of creation.

Isis joined forces with the god Thoth and together they cared for the earth people, teaching man agriculture, medicine, and the secrets of magick. She was also skilled in healing. It is said that it was Isis who invented the rites of embalming for which the Egyptians were famous. She was also responsible, as the counterpart of Osiris, for teaching women weaving and spinning, and how to grind corn. Her strongest appeal was as the mourning widow and devoted mother; every woman could identify with Isis and she has been seen by many through the ages as the archetypal woman.

Her great magickal powers were spoken of much in ancient times. It is said that Isis may have been more powerful than Osiris and even the supreme god Ra.

After all, using her powerful magick, she did trick Ra into revealing his secret name to her, which then gave her power over him. Yet, Isis is never portrayed as selfish or cruel, except of course to those who would seek to harm those she loved.

On the Path to Isis you will hear your magickal name that will take on a more spiritual function. Your magickal name can connect you more closely with the divine. While it is true to say that there are still many people for whom magickal names offer a feeling of security and anonymity, most people choose to use them for a more spiritual meaning.

On many of the paths, you will be shown symbols and given objects to use, such as the ankh, the looped cross of Egypt, which Isis carries as supreme initiatrix. This may account for the oddly shaped sceptres held by the Black Virgins. According to the alchemist, their very blackness and greenness points to the beginning of the opus, whose secret is to be found in "the sex of Isis." She is sometimes depicted wearing the colour green even though in the early dynasties the ancient Egyptians didn't know the art of producing green dye.

Isis always displayed power and compassion, and although she was crafty, she was also forgiving. Isis symbolizes *all* the qualities of women. All feminine archetypes in all legends are linked to one soul, be they goddesses, the Virgin Mary, or priestesses of all kinds and persuasions. They are all of the same spirit essence.

In ancient Khemit, the goddess's name was Auset, which means "exceeding queen" or simply "spirit."

She is one of the oldest deities in Egypt, and certainly the oldest to survive the ages in much the same form. To some, she may also be the most important, for although the other gods were worshipped widely, all ancient Egyptians honoured her almost universally, and indeed, Isis followers are still found today.

Her fame quickly spread to all corners of the Roman Empire. There was even a temple to Isis on the River Thames in Southwark, London. But her most famous temple is to be found in Philae in Aswan.

By the late Egyptian dynasties, Isis had become the most important and the most powerful magickal deity of the Egyptian pantheon. Magick was core to the entire legend of Isis, certainly more so than any other Egyptian deity.

Isis celebrates the River Nile. Her tears are a renewal of life and fertility. She is the perfume of life and light. She is the island garden that springs from the Nile, an oasis of life, where time stands still. The more powerful provinces insisted on the adoption of their time-honoured conceptions. Views of the trinity in accordance with the Egyptian traditions were established. Not only was the adoration of Isis under a new name restored, but also even her image, standing on the crescent moon, reappeared. The well-known effigy of that goddess with the infant Horus in her arms has descended to our days, in the beautiful artistic creations of the "Madonna and child."

If the Virgin Mary has her nuns, who are consecrated to her and bound to live in chastity, so had Isis her priestesses in Egypt, as Vesta had hers at Rome, and the Hindu Nari, "mother of the world," hers also. The virgins consecrated to her cults—the Devadasi of the temples, who were the nuns of the days of old—lived in great chastity, and were objects of the most extraordinary veneration, as were the holy women of the goddess.

In the tomb of Rameses II, in the valley of Biban-el-Molouk, in western Thebes, Champollion Jnr discovered a wall painting and, according to him, it was the most ancient ever yet found. It represents the heavens symbolized by the figure of a woman bedecked with stars. The birth of the sun is figured by the form of a little child, issuing from the bosom of its "divine mother."

The devotees of Isis regarded her as a Virgin Mother when holding her infant son Horus in her arms. In some statues and bas-reliefs, when she appears alone she is either completely nude or veiled from head to foot. But in the Mysteries, in common with nearly every other goddess, she is entirely veiled from head to foot, as a symbol of a mother's chastity.

The most familiar of all statues that have survived shows Isis holding her son Horus to her breast. It is a classic pose, which is repeated in Christianity; the only difference is that Isis and Horus are replaced by Mary and the infant Jesus.

PATH TO ISIS
Journey to Philae

Don your white robe and tie a red cord around your waist. This will be in respect of the Neter you will be working with.

Build your pylon; visualise the grand structure pushing up through the earth, towering towards the sky, and disappearing into the heavens. Touch each stone and examine each incised hieroglyph. Feel the warmth of the sunlight as it caresses the pale gold sandstone blocks, soon turning into coolness as you pass through the shaded portal. On the lintel of the portal, hieroglyphs of Isis appear.

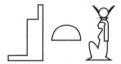

Commit them to memory. This symbol is charged; look at each mark and take it within. This is your gateway that will take you to the heart of her temple. You will learn how to focus on its energy as you are drawn in.

It is early morning and the land is shrouded in mist that rapidly dissipates as the golden rays of Ra burn it off. As you contemplate the splendour around you, a figure that has the head of an ibis catches your attention. It is Djehuty, god of writing and knowledge. He is also god of secrets and magickal spells. But most important of all, he is a "time lord."

You stand transfixed as he pulls himself to his full height, straightening out the many creases in the folds of his black-skinned neck.

This bird-beaked dignitary looks back at you through amber eyes that shine with little sparks of yellow. They hold an insight gifted to him long before Chaos birthed the sacred Mound. You blink suddenly, not believing what you see, and in that split second of you closing your eyes, he has transformed his ibis head into that of a man, but still with the same warm amber eyes that match the warmth of his smile.

On his head he wears a wig of fine strands of lapis lazuli linked together with filaments of gold. Around his neck is a collar made of turquoise and dark blue faïence beads. He wears a short kilt of pleated pale blue linen edged with silver. The colours contrast with the gold colour of his skin that gleams in the early light of the morning. There is a radiance about him that instils trust in you. He will be your guide and protector as you journey through the ancient land of Khemit, and along the many paths to the Neters.

You walk with Djehuty along a dust track that leads to the river where a boatman is waiting to take you to the small island called P'aaleq, the "Remote Place" in ancient Egyptian, where stands the amazing Temple of Isis.

As you board the craft, Djehuty gives you the customary token, which you pass to the boatman in payment for your passage. The rising vapours from the water cleanse you as you pull away from the riverbank.

The crossing is made in silence as the boat cuts through the calm water that sparkles like diamonds on the inky blue of the river dedicated to the Nile god Hapy. It is incredible to think that just beyond these tranquil waters the river gathers speed, dropping twenty feet in swirling eddies and whirlpools, giving way to turbulent falls of white water that rip through the sandy gorges for a distance of thirty miles. Many pharaohs attempted to tame these waters and provide a better passage around these rapids— but failed.

The mist clears as you arrive at the island, a granite outcrop that must have been originally chosen as an embodiment of the primeval hill on which the first temple was said to have rested.

The boatman steadies his craft at a small jetty and you alight, walking up steps worn by the passage of time and the countless travellers gone before you.

Lovely are the doorways in Philae, enticing are the shallow steps that lead you onward and upward; gracious yellow towers seem to smile a quiet welcome.

Djehuty guides you into the Outer Courtyard flanked by the eastern and western colonnades, a veritable forest of pillars that stand testament to an age gone by. You pass the chapels to Imhotep and the Nubian deities Arensnuphis and Mandulis.

By now several travellers have come to pay homage to the goddess and leave tokens with the priesthood, who will make libations and say special prayers for their safe passage through the dangerous territory beyond their southern borders to the "Land of Ghosts."

Djehuty now leads the way and you continue across the courtyard towards the first pylon and up five steps that lead to the left-most door, which is the Mamissi. Two granite lions flank the portal.

Before entering, you stand in front of the entrance and gaze up at the carefully incised wall relief depicting priests carrying the barque of Isis. The temple is shot with radiant light that falls on the stone, almost bringing to life the beautiful form of the goddess as she floats on high. The colours vibrate with an inner life, a wonderful green, coral pink, a lapis blue as deep as the blue of the Nile, and the lustrous fiery red of Ra. In Philae, one is wrapped in a radiance of colour, for those who painted these capitals and walls painted for the greater glory of Isis.

Being in Philae is like being in a delicate dream. It represents a certain delicious femininity that seduces your eyes and your heart. The walls become the psychic circle of protection imbued with their own power. Is it the spirit of Isis you feel?

Taking a deep breath, you walk through the darkened portal, and as you do you hear a baby's crying as it enters the world. You look around in curiosity and then realise the Mamissi is the Birth House dedicated to Horus, son of Isis. Djehuty waits patiently for you in the Inner Court, then, together you walk towards a row of five rooms, each with two stories.

One of these rooms is being used as a laboratory for making the precious incense for the temple workings. You pause to watch a priest as he distills oils from flowers; the aroma of lotus, rose, and orange blossom hangs heavy in the morning air. Your presence does not seem to disturb him at all; he just looks up at you and smiles, his bright eyes full of life. It strikes you that this all-embracing joy of life seems to greet you at every stage. It is vibrant and passionate.

You move on to the next room and watch priests and scribes milling about, some carrying manuscripts, others writing-trays. They are so absorbed in their work, your presence at the door goes unnoticed. On the walls of this chamber are depictions of Djehuty himself, in his form of the ibis whom you now recognise. The colours stand out in sharp contrast on the smooth white-washed walls.

Beautiful music is filling the air, turning your gaze to the pillar heads that face the Inner Court. They carry the face of the goddess Het-Hert, or Hathor, mistress of song. You close your eyes and listen to the delicate plucking of a harp, but within the sounds dwells something else—what is it? A murmur or a perfumed breath? The temple lives!

Excitement fills you as you walk through the first antechamber, but you are suddenly stopped by a priest who asks you to remove your footwear before going any farther. He then instructs you to wash your hands and face before giving you a white linen robe that smells like freshly cut grass and morning sunshine. He then gives you a red sash to tie around your waist, the sign of Isis. Your forehead is anointed with oil of frankincense. You then rinse your mouth with natron water that tastes quite strange.

You collect your thoughts in preparation for your entry into the realm of Isis. Your heart picks up a faster rhythm; is it nerves or hopeful anticipation?

Two more rooms in a row lead you towards the sanctum. At this point you are very nervous, but are calmed when you see that the walls around you are alive with wondrous scenes of Isis suckling the baby Horus in the marshes of Chemmis. As you take in this image, think of how Isis nursing Horus gave way to the Virgin and the Child, and see the cycles spin away, ringing the changes as Egypt's time passes, paving the way for Christianity.

Your eyes now rest on the figure of Horus wearing the double crown of Khemit. Your attention is broken by a fluttering of wings...it is Nekhbet, the vulture goddess. There she is, high up in the roof, spreading and folding her wings, her predatory eyes watching your every move.

The air around you is chilled. The Mamissi is a living, breathing world that is drawing you ever deeper and deeper, altering your very states of consciousness and awareness.

Before you is the entrance to the inner sanctum of Isis but you find that you are unable to enter. You can see through the portal but there is an invisible force that bars your entry. You look nervously around, wondering what is stopping you from entering. A voice tells you to cast your mind back to the very reason why you are here in the first place. To be thrilled by the sight of a goddess, to bathe in her beauty, or to learn the secrets within yourself?

Djehuty steps in front of the door and, with a grand sweep of his right hand, he forms a sign of an ankh in the air. The sign dissolves the force field between you and the sanctum beyond. He looks at you and says:

"From this moment on, O pilgrim, commit this sign to your memory and use it to enter all your paths to the Neters. To enter this sacred place and lay eyes upon the goddess is only for the High Priest whilst conducting the daily services."

As if very far off, you hear the solemn chanting of priests. But are they chanting, or is it a lament? Was it not here that a decree was sent forth from Constantinople that all Egypt should be Christian? And the priests of the sacred brotherhood of Isis were driven from their temple?

That all-pervading aroma of lotus, rose, and orange blossom wafts around you. The goddess is now very close. A pale blue haze fills the chamber and you strain your eyes to look through it. It is as if an electric current is sweeping across your skin, and you shiver at the sensation. Then you see the long aquiline nose and face of Isis.

She sits before you on a rich purple throne in all her magnificent glory. Her fragrance is of a mother. Her aroma of rose and orange blossom, now intermingled with a hint of sandalwood, inspires comfort, beauty, abundance, communion, and harmony. Your fears fall away from you at this instant.

The goddess's white diaphanous robe and red sash moves gently as Nekhbet continues slowly flapping her wings above you. On her head, Isis wears the horned sun headdress held in place by a coronet of golden cobras that glisten with a life of their own. Her ebony black hair hangs long and straight over her shoulders; her smooth scented skin is the colour of pale copper. She is full of sexual guile. On her forehead, she wears the electrum circlet shot with gold and silver.

Her eyes are outlined in kohl, emphasising the liquid blue of their colour. Her lips are carmine; her face shines. She is indeed far more beautiful than legend has portrayed and it is not a cold beauty, but one shimmering with colour and light. Her eyes patiently behold you.

A heavy golden collar decorated with a lapis lazuli-jewelled lotus hangs around her delicate neck. In her right hand, she holds a golden Djed staff that represents the backbone of her beloved Osiris.

Nestled against her left knee is her naked child, Horus. The golden-skinned child is quite unaware of your presence and is more intent in pressing his right toe on the tail of a red snake that is coiling up the staff held by his mother. The serpent represents knowledge, and Horus is demonstrating to you that he is in control. He smiles as the serpent tries to escape. Horus's head is shaved completely except for one long antet, the "side lock of youth," on the right side of his head.

You stand there awestruck, just drinking in the atmosphere around you, not knowing what to do or say. It is as if Isis has enveloped you in her arms. Her hair is soft about you, and when she speaks, it is like the voice of the first mother.

All around you sistra are being shaken, and that far-off chanting continues. Then walls begin to dissolve around the goddess and her child as stone gives way to a landscape of papyrus and marsh where Isis hid from her brother Set during the birth of her son. Then the goddess raises her Djed staff and all is silenced.

Isis speaks. Her voice is likened to a soft breeze, both warm and refreshing, and she energises you with her words:

"I am she who triumphed over death to bring my beloved husband-brother back to life. I am mistress of the sun and daughter of the lord gods. I am wife of a king and carried the young god within me to this sacred place and gave birth to him. I am Isis, great mother of gods, and Queen of the Mamissi. Look upon me as I truly am, unfettered by your hopes and fantasies. I have lingered in the shadows watching you shape and unshape me age after age, an empty image not worthy of my Name. I am Power, I am Love, I am Eternity. Remember this, my child. Through me shall you find the greater mysteries of Life. I speak of many things which are known and unknown, my breath to your breath, my heart to your heart."

The pale blue haze that filled the sanctum is now fading but her beautiful form continues to shimmer. In front of the goddess is an altar of pure crystal. On it is a bowl of electric-blue glass that contains the perpetual flame found on all the altars of the sacred mystery schools. Next to the flame is an emerald goblet filled with amber liquid, an incense burner, and an ankh carved out of black onyx. Each object vibrates with its own energy.

The child steps away from his mother, picks up the goblet, and passes it to you. As he does so, the red serpent at his feet uncurls its form and slithers up his arm and winds its way across to yours. You look into the eyes of the smiling child and smile in return, innately understanding the significance of that moment. In perfect trust, you sip the liquid. An inner voice tells you this is the elixir of life that will serve to feed your imagination as you journey through the ancient land of Khemit.

Horus reaches up and, with both hands, takes the goblet and replaces it back on the altar. You are then instructed to place your fingertips on the crystal altar and inhale the incense deeply, then exhale slowly. The incense is sweet and very heady. This will serve to cleanse the senses and heighten your awareness in building your astral temple. As you inhale, you are breathing in the very breath of the goddess who has made it holy. Feel a wave of pure harmony wash over your core of being. Even the pale blue haze has a life of its own. It whispers:

"If the essence and perfection of all good are comprehended in the goddess, and if you adhere to a more excellent nature, you will obtain a union with her, the contemplation of truth, and the possession of intellect. A knowledge of all the gods is accompanied with a conversion to, and knowledge of, yourself."

Isis speaks:

"I have allowed you to gaze upon me in my guise as White Isis, but I also have a dark and veiled side, where I am known as the Black Isis, the Auset of mystery and magick that exists only as a memory in the most ancient of Khemit lore. But the black and the white exist within you; all you have to do is pick up the black ankh, the key, whereby you will unlock a barrier to a further mystery within."

You inwardly digest what Isis has said. Dare you take the next step? Let not fear of your own darkness cloud the path to insight and self-knowledge. Think clearly, for this is the moment of your coming into being; through sacrifice and death comes the dawn and rebirth.

After a while, you reach forward to pick up the black ankh, and as you do, Isis and Horus vanish into the pale blue haze, but it gives off just enough light for you to see around the chamber. Gone is marsh and papyrus as the walls become stone again. You seem to be going in circles as you wander about. It is said that when the pharaoh proceeds through the temple, the cosmic circles are repeated on earth. Without this celebration, Life would not be maintained. Everything in existence is returning back to the source from whence it came, back to she who gives birth to the god.

Suddenly you see on the northern wall of the chamber a deeply cut impression of an ankh of the same proportions as the one you hold. Instinct tells you to press one on top of the other, and as you do, the wall vibrates and sings. The pitch of this tune enthralls you, and as you concentrate on the notes you hear embedded in the resonance your secret name. Meditate: open yourself up to messages about what your name should be. Spend some time contemplating why you are on this path. Often nature will leave us clues along the way. You relearn the magick of your name and the mystery of its sound. Thus your name becomes the password that bridges earth, sky, and heaven.

The wall dissolves, revealing a sloping passageway leading under this temple to another place. You hear the gush of an underground stream, but could this be possible? Djehuty is behind you lighting your way with a flaming torch.

You halt as you come to the end of the passage and Djehuty raises his right hand, forming the sign of the ankh in the air. Another doorway opens. You are standing on the threshold of a temple created out of the living rock. You sense that it is older than Khemit itself and would have belonged to the black Hamatic people who lived in Khemit long before the red Egyptians inhabited the land. You enter this temple followed by your guardian.

Above your head burns the perpetual flame, revealing a large chamber. At the far end, seated upon a throne of black basalt is the veiled-faced figure of a woman. The air is saturated with the heady scent of cinnamon mingled with myrrh and amber, your lungs are now heavy as you draw it in. Your blood sings with an intensity you did not think was possible. Who is this woman? You can just make out that her features are pure Negroid. She is robed in sheer gossamer of spun silver that resembles moonlight. In her left hand ,she holds a staff with an ancient totem you cannot make out. This goddess is so very different from the other aspect of her being. Before her is an altar smeared with the blood of sacrifice! The silence around you stretches into eternity; it swirls and eddies then captures you in its grip. An unknown force propels you into the Great Void and from within its vastness a presence reaches out. From out of the inky blackness of the Eternal Night she emerges, veiled in shadows and resplendent in primeval power.

You stand there spellbound as her dark eyes pierce your very soul, and a chill sinks into your core. Then she speaks to you, her voice warm and rich:

"Be not afraid, my child, for what you see is the dark side of your soul. I seek not your death, as I readily hold off death for my faithful followers, for I am the all-powerful Auset! I alone will overcome fate.

"And if you show yourself obedient to my divinity then you will know that I alone have permitted you to extend your life beyond the time allotted you by destiny."

Mark her words well. They will serve to fulfill your fate.

As the goddess Auset raises her staff, the sacrificial altar is washed clean by the waters of the underground stream. On it is an empty box crafted out of fine queen ebony. The red streaks in the wood resemble blood mingling with the black mother, her womb reabsorbing the blood and flesh of her children.

You wish you could lift the veil from the goddess's face. Your desire wells up from the depths of your soul. She reads your mind and answers:

"I wear the veil as a vow of silence and secrecy." With her right hand, she points towards the box and asks you to cast into it a spiritual sacrifice. This is the moment to put aside any doubts or fears that will inhibit your spiritual development as you walk along your chosen path.

It is a very private moment as you step forward to look deep into the veiled face of the goddess. The aroma around her is likened to a fragrance of a garden in moonlight, jasmine and magnolia. You take deep inhalations, breathing in her very breath. Then, looking into the box, you make your sacrifice. She smiles as the lid of the box slowly closes. You suddenly feel strengthened, as if you have rid yourself of a heavy load. A deep knowingness descends upon you. All is clear now. Your eyes shine with an intensity that pierces the darkness of the Veil. It is as if you had spent an aeon in the Mother's womb, lost in thoughts, in whispers and dreams: consciousness dissolving into unconsciousness. Then, a faint heartbeat echoes through the darkness. Life is flowing back into your veins. She gives back your existence.

As Auset speaks, a blood-red glow fills the temple:

"You shall live in blessing, you shall live glorious in my protection; and when you have fulfilled your allotted span of life and descended into the underworld, there too you shall see me, as you are seeing me now, shining."

As you prepare to leave the temple, Djehuty is there by your side smiling, and in your right hand he places an ankh. He tells you to use it wisely. You may return whenever you have a need to be with the goddess. A door opens and you leave this temple of Auset, the land of dreams, where among the hidden ways your soul has been lost in magick. You construct your pylons and walk through the portal to your world of familiar regions. Utter your secret name to the gods and seal the door behind you. Yes, you have left Philae, but it will never fade from your mind.

TWO

LEGEND OF SOBEK AND HARWER

I bow down to your (Sobek and Harwer) names
May they be my physician
May they drive away pain from me

STATUE INSCRIPTION OF MONTEMHET, THIRD INTERMEDIATE PERIOD

Sobek was one of the oldest of the Egyptian gods. In the Fayoum, as well as at Kom Ombos, he was worshipped since the pre-dynastic times, and there, in the holy lake of his temple, were great numbers of holy crocodiles, which Strabo tells us were decorated with jewels like pretty women.

The temple was located in the ancient city of Pa-Sobek, "Domain of Sobek," and stands on a headland at a bend on the River Nile. It provides one of the most spectacular settings of any of Egypt's river temples.

Kom Ombos Temple is not just unusual, but unique. The ground plan is the result of the unification of two adjacent temples, each dedicated to a different divinity: the crocodile-headed Sobek, "He who finds," and Harwer, an ancient falcon-headed Neter and solar war god.

This is the reason why the temple was called both Pr' Sobek, "House of the Crocodile," and Pr' Heru, "House of the Falcon." An imaginary line divides the temple longitudinally into two parts, each with its own entrance, Hypostyle Halls, chapels, and shrines.

The right part of the temple was consecrated to Sobek, and the left to Harwer, whose winged disk that protects from all evils is depicted over all the entrance portals. This temple was the work of the Ptolemies, who built it on the site of a much older and smaller double sanctuary of which little remains, but nevertheless echoes the dual aspect of the first temple. It was the intent of the original builders to create not just a house to be shared by two gods, but a vessel whereby we mortals could actually enter our own brain.

The dual aspect is the left and right of the brain; Sobek is given the right chamber that signifies the "animal brain" and analyzes the environment for the sights and sounds useful for survival. In essence, animals are almost one hundred percent "right-brained."

Animals must be very concerned about their visual environment, both for food and danger. Therefore, this area is one of the oldest and best-developed areas of the brain. Most animals can see shape, colour, motion perception, and depth perception.

Humans have kept the animal talents on the right side, but have adapted the left brain for language and tool use.

Vision in the human left brain is specialized for reading. The left brain learns to see arrangements of lines we call alphabet letters.

The ancient Egyptians first noticed that the right brain tended to control the left side of the body and the left brain tends to control the right side of the body.

Although each hemisphere is almost identical in terms of structure, each operates in an entirely different way and is associated with very different activities. This is known as specialization or lateralization.

The Path to Sobek and Harwer is one of the most important, as it leads you through an imprint of the human brain. When we experience a magickal journey we become excited, our pulse rate increases, and our blood pressure drops. Our breathing is altered and we take large volumes of oxygen and life-force into the bloodstream and, because of its excellent blood supply, the pineal gland receives much stimulation from the oxygen-drenched blood, causing it to vibrate, thereby stimulating the release of our body's own psychedelic chemical. The ancients regarded the pineal gland as the "holy of holies," the gateway into the soul; an energy vortex; a meeting place between soul and body.

The left side of the temple is dedicated to Harwer, god of victory and also known as "the good doctor." Kom Ombos became famous for its healing power and was a major pilgrimage site where a healing cult developed. The temple was a sanctuary for many patients who were seeking help and treatment by the priests. On these occasions, the priests would gather in the temple precinct and spend many days and nights fasting and in prayer. The fasting consisted of abstaining from all pleasures of the table, eating of no living thing, and drinking no wine. This would alter the chemistry in their brain, and in so doing produce a trancelike state.

In a side chapel is a festival calendar, which would have been used by the ancient Egyptians to record all religious events occurring throughout the year.

As in the ancient land of Khemit, it has been found that the great religious holy days of all faiths tend to cluster around the times of the solstices and equinoxes. It is possible that the human pineal gland responds to the changes in the length of daylight, and by changing the balance of what are termed neurohumors in the brain, this perhaps affects a great incidence of psychedelic states in vulnerable individuals just at these crucial times. Incidentally, the festival day for Sobek falls on the twenty-first day of Koiak, which also happens to be the autumn equinox.

Without light, there would be no life on earth. Light is received by the sun, which is also the greatest heat source and energy provider in our solar system. All the ancient cultures knew about the sun's healing power. The Egyptians, for example, used dyed cloth to cover wounds and coloured crystals for healing purposes.

The priests of Kom Ombos knew that as light and colours enter our bodies through the eyes, the skin, and the food we eat, even the clothes we wear have a profound effect on our well-being. They knew that looking at and focussing on colours stimulates the whole body.

Scientific tests have now been able to verify what ancient cultures have known for centuries: that some colours have a stimulating, energising, and vibrant effect like red, orange, and yellow; and other colours have a soothing, calming, and relaxing effect like green and blue; and looking at grey has a suppressing effect on us.

This path is the path of balance where you, the initiate, will demonstrate your ability to balance the polarities of the left and right brain. You will travel from the pit of darkness into the light of awareness. Here you will learn to master your emotions through love from the heart.

PATH TO SOBEK AND HARWER
Journey to Kom Ombos

Don your white robe and tie purple and yellow cords around your waist. This will be in respect of the Neters you will be working with.

Build your pylons and make the sign of the ankh in the air above your head. On the lintel of the portal, hieroglyphs of Sobek and Harwer appear:

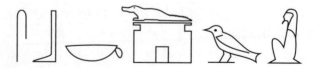

Commit them to memory. These symbols are charged; look at each mark and take it within. As you utter your secret name ,your journey takes you to the realm of Sobek and Harwer, Horus the Elder. You will learn how to focus on their energy as you are drawn in.

A shower of golden light greets you; full and voluptuous and beautiful, it swirls and eddies around and through you. Embedded within that light is a multitude of sounds that sharpen to become voices. Voices calling, but who are they calling? The voices disappear into the depths of the magnificent double-entranced temple that has appeared before you, and you eagerly make your way towards it. But Djehuty hurries towards you saying:

"Pilgrim, do not enter yet! Come, let us go first to the holy lake. I have wondrous sights to show you."

You walk with your guardian along the banks of the river Nile until you reach a smaller temple bordering a lake. Before you is a group of priests who are feeding and lovingly coaxing the sacred crocodiles to emerge from the water. The melodious voices of the priests ring out in the clear morning light, hypnotic and strangely soothing, as you hear them saying:

"Come, my beauties, come and let us scrub clean your scaly bodies."

These sounds sink deep within your mind and reverberate throughout its labyrinthine tunnels, stirring ancient memories. Awakening from your reverie, you marvel at the sight of these creatures that slowly and elegantly slither from their watery depths. You marvel at the fact that they allow such intimate contact from the priests. Djehuty says quietly:

"In life, the children of Sobek are worshipped by the people of Kom Ombos and even unto death these reptiles are considered sacred. Before embalming, the oil of messeh is taken from their bodies, refined, and then used for anointing the kings of Egypt at the time of their coronation. This oil, and only this oil, confers the mark of true kingship. Priests and other royal monarchs right up to your present day will adopt the practice of anointing."

Your guardian lifts his head and appears transfixed, as if a message is being communicated to him. He looks down at you and nods.

"Come, let us not tarry here. I must get you to the main temple for your working."

You both enter the temple precinct from the eastern side through an ancient gate and pass another small temple that is dedicated to the Neter Hathor. The sound of a reed flute offers up an ancient tune, a rhythm that is then taken up by the chanting of women's voices, so simple, yet so powerful in its effect. You want to linger but cannot, mindful of the importance of the experience that is to come.

Soon the temple appears within your sight. Going through the forecourt, you are greeted by the double entrances you previously noticed. Each leads to one half of the temple dedicated to the twin deities Sobek and Harwer. The theme of duality is as always echoed in the many aspects of Khemit. Is this an indication of what is to come? Reconciliation of the Two into One; light with dark, past with present? Being with nonbeing? We shall see...

Djehuty leads you to the second Hypostyle Hall that also has twin entrances and fifteen columns; five of them are incorporated in the front wall that shows Ptolemy VII holding hymnal texts before Sobek and Harwer.

You look above at the tall columns shaped like palm trees and terminated in capitals in the form of leaves girdled with lapis lazuli and gold and topped with bas-relief of geese. Marble and alabaster, granite of different colours finish the walls. The aroma of lotus, frankincense, and amber incense fills the halls.

You continue walking through the temple and come to three double-entrance vestibules, each one a different colour. The atmosphere in each of these vestibules pulses to a particular vibratory rate, difficult to express but felt profoundly on a cellular level. Their walls sparkle with jewel brightness. You are curious to know what it is that makes them gleam so, but are interrupted by a group of men and women who are now approaching. They all come looking for special healing at this temple. They range from all age groups and all levels of society, yet are unified by one desire. Djehuty suggests that you join these pilgrims as they are about to be healed by priests who have been specially trained; each one has a rare and particular gift.

Several have remained to be treated individually, so you join a group and are ushered by a priest who leads you to the perimeter corridor directly at the back of the double shrines.

A faceted crystal is then given to each member, and as you take yours, you wonder why. Your guardian Djehuty murmurs:

"All will be clear soon."

As you are about to leave, you notice another group of priests who have begun a monotone chant as they proceed solemnly into the middle chamber that is out of bounds except for the initiated and Pharaoh. Their chanting is beginning to have a strange effect on the crystal you hold in your hand. It literally begins to throb; each "breath" gathers the sacred essence flowing through the temple and channels it into you, charging notions that symbolize the duality of your higher and lower natures, all to be balanced in perfect harmony.

As you link up with the group and slowly walk in a single line along the inner side of the back wall of the temple, you are aware that the crystals held by those around you are simultaneously charging and pulsating.

The corridor before you is long and narrow and, although dark, it is cleverly lit by white gauze-covered lanterns giving one the illusion of being inside a long opalescent shell.

On the inner side of the back wall of the temple is a remarkable scene; medical instruments are being presented to a seated god who is bestowing a blessing upon them.

Imperceptibly you begin to feel lighter as if layer upon layer of your very being—notion of selfhood, identity, call it what you may—this layer is being shed with each step. All is then reabsorbed into the matrix of the temple.

Each member of the group, including you, is given a choice of coloured strips of linen to tie around your forehead: red, yellow, blue, purple, or white. Listen to what your body tells you is needed, and choose that colour.

As you tie the strip of linen around your forehead, the vibration of the colour is impacting on your inner being, linking to your deeper self. Light and colour are entering your body.

The priests are now chanting at different rhythms, causing you to drift high above the corridor, the different frequencies impacting indelibly upon your brain. Your consciousness undergoes a process of transformation. From the material world, you are projected through an immense gateway into a space that is filled with darkness; this gradually clears to reveal the temple in plan, but it is not the temple you see; it is your brain. There on the right is Sobek invoking special awareness, the magnificence of colour, your imagination, and the ability to daydream. On the left side of your brain sits Harwer, who is responsible for the power of your speech and use of words. He is imparting your ability to analyse and use logic and numbers. Time has no meaning within this space; minutes or aeons could have passed and you would not care. So much knowledge to absorb and it was lost to an unawakened humanity. The tragedy of it!

You hear yourself saying: "I want more! I want the key that opens up my back brain; I want all the knowledge I once knew to pour forth. I want to free that part of my brain that has shut down. It feels as if I have waited an eternity to come to this point. Do not take it away from me now, please!"

All are looking up at you in silence as your body now makes its journey down, but it is not the corridor you're earthed to; it is the point midway between the two shrines. This is a place where god and human meet face to face.

Djehuty is there, standing right in front of you, holding your two hands, which still cup the crystal that is glowing through your skin, showing every vein, bone, and mark. The guardian closes his eyes and speaks in a tongue lost even to the ancients. Incantations glide from his tongue. Thoughts are transformed into sounds. Your molecules rearrange themselves in response to the energetic shift within the crystal. Regeneration and rejuvenation of Self occurs. All this soon fades into the background as Sobek and Harwer speak in unison behind you, but it is not their voices you hear; it is the sound within your brain. It is saying:

"When our brother Lord Anpu readies you for the realm beyond, he takes from your mortal body the many organs that are kept in the sacred canopic jars, guarded by the sons of Heru. But we touch not your brain as it is the Holy of Holies and it rests for always within your temple. To disturb the brain would be to disturb every Neter who rests in each location, both on the left and the right. There are actually places within your living brain where the priesthood travel to be taught by us. You have no need of a key, for we are there always to teach you and guide you, when you are ready to receive the sacred knowledge. Enter favoured and leave beloved."

Your guardian escorts you through the temple where you construct your pylons and walk through the portal to your world of familiar regions. Utter your secret name and close the gate behind you.

THREE

LEGEND OF HORUS THE ELDER

... He is Horus who arose as king of Upper and Lower Egypt,
who united the Two Lands in the Nome of the Wall,
the place in which the Two Lands were united.

FROM THE SHABAKA STONE, BRITISH MUSEUM

This most ancient of deities is most definitely not to be confused with Horus (Hor-sa-Isis or Haroeris), child of Isis and Osiris. In his earliest incarnation, Horus was a sky god whose name was "Hor," meaning either "face" or "distant," but he later evolved into a solar deity during the introduction of the Osirian cult.

The usual iconography of this god was of either a falcon or a man with the head of a falcon on his shoulders. However this Neter embodied within himself a multitude of falcon gods in various manifestations and with various names, a few being:

Horus of Behdet (located in the Western Delta) took form as a hawk-headed warrior. His cult moved from the Western Delta to Edfu, in Upper Egypt in later times, and the temple here subsequently became known famously as Edfu. It was known colloquially as Djeba ("Retribution Town") because of the fact that Set and his followers were brought to justice there.

Harakhti ("Horus of the Two Horizons"). God of the east and the rising sun.

Behdety ("He of [the] behdet"). The hawk-winged sun disk which symbolised the passage of the sun through the sky.

Harpocrates (Har-pa-khered—"Horus the child"). The god manifests as a child sitting on his mother's knee, wearing the side-lock of hair and occasionally sucking his fingers. This form is of the divine child.

Harisiese (Horus, the Son of Isis). This representation symbolises the legitimacy of the Osirian line made manifest in the off-spring of Isis and Osiris.

Horus or Heru was evident as a Neter of kings from at least predynastic times, with a cult centre based in the ancient capital city of Upper Egypt, Nekhen (Greek name Hierakonopolis—"City of the Falcon"). A falcon deity had been preeminent in Nekhen since early times and it was this deity, Nekheny, who was subsequently absorbed into Horus. Nekhen's crown was lost to Edfu in later times, but it still remained an important cult centre for Horus.

Excavations at this site in modern times have revealed an oval templelike structure (dating to the early Naqada II) closely resembling temples found in Mesopotamia, perhaps indicating ancient trade links with this culture. The peoples of the ancient world were great explorers; they exchanged not only goods but also ideas. These ideas were like precious seeds that gave rise to important cultural, spiritual, and economic developments, and Egypt's civilisation benefited greatly from the flow of this information.

Remains at this site have revealed a circular stone wall, paved areas, and remnants of column bases. We can only surmise that a pole displaying the image of the Neter may have stood in the centre of this space, whilst at its base were ceremonial platforms and around the courtyard were workshops for a variety of craftsmen. The central shrine looks to consist of three rooms, with four huge timber pillars making up the façade and coloured mats serving as the walls.

With regard to the relationship between Horus and Set, we need to be aware of the dynamics of the relationship between the Neters and their embodiment of balanced rulership within the Two Lands. There has been great debate about whether there is a historical basis to the Horus-Set struggle enshrined within Egyptian mythology. Some authorities see it as a predynastic power struggle between the tribal leaders of Upper Egypt (followers of Horus) and those of Lower Egypt (followers of Set). Once unification had occurred, Horus reigned supreme as national deity, and history was rewritten by the victors many decades later.

We may be familiar with the tales of Horus, son of Isis, and the titanic battle with his uncle Set for the throne of Egypt, so we shall not enter into its recounting here.

Have we come any nearer to even understanding this Neter? Perhaps? Or perhaps not. As an embodiment of divine and human kingship, Horus emanates measured calm, deep wisdom, and immense strength. He is a warrior king embodying the power and beauty of an ancient, ancient civilisation, one who is capable of great ferocity in defence, but it is a controlled force, wasting nothing, focused and direct. Equally he is wise in the ways of kingship, one who is utterly trustworthy and speaks words of Truth.

It is to our discredit that our perceptions of this most ancient and august of Neters appears not to shift too far from the image of the Osirian child. That may be so, Pilgrim, but you are blessed with free will; seek the truth behind the illusionary truths that confront you.

PATH TO HORUS THE ELDER
Journey to Edfu

Don your white robe and tie a yellow cord around your waist. This will be in respect of the Neter you will be working with.

Build your pylons and make the sign of the ankh in the air above your head. On the lintel of the portal, hieroglyphs of Horus appear.

Commit them to memory. This symbol is charged; look at each mark and take it within. As you utter your secret name, your journey takes you to the Temple of Edfu, where you will commune with Horus the Elder. This is a gateway that will take you to the heart of his realm. You will learn how to focus on his energy as you are drawn in.

A primeval light saturates the sky in the east. You watch tendrils of gold spread throughout the dawn sky; it fills you with new vigour and energy. Something is stirring, as far off across the sands you feel the gathering of great spirits, but see nothing for the moment. Then through the eternal silence an awesome note reaches your ears. It sounds as if it began from the dawn of time, a time before the gods existed. It then fades to an echo. You strain your ears to catch the last strains of this call, so familiar yet so brief!

Through a haze on the horizon wanders a lonely bird. His spindly legs and long black beak tell you it is your guardian Djehuty, and you welcome his presence, raising your hand and waving. But as if watching a far-off, quivering mirage, you lose him in some wayward dream. He appears absorbed in some urgent task, casting not a glance at your face. You drop your hand to find again the desert sand is your only companion. You stand in silence amid the dunes, like the sands of time, forever moving, revealing their secrets only to those who are worthy. Are you worthy, Pilgrim and seeker of the ancient mysteries?

The wind stirs the sand around you and gently caresses your robe as it snakes round your ankles. You suddenly hold your breath as the sands rise under your feet, forming a gigantic primeval mound. Suddenly your guardian materialises by your side in the company of the Seven Sages, who are attended by two enigmatic gods known as Wa and Aa.

Djehuty holds a stylus and palette in his hands in readiness for dictation. He pays no attention to you, then begins busily designing structures, calculating each line with incredible speed. As he draws, huge masonry shapes explode out of the sands around the mound. His companions look on silently, mentally orchestrating each stage. They are strange beings; their very gazes upon the now-forming temple walls burn inscriptions that tell a story about the Zep Tepi, which was the very first prehistoric Egyptian civilisation.

"But who *are* you?" you ask, trying to hear their words that are now pulsating wave-forms that travel through the air towards your ears:

"We are the founders; you know us as divine beings. We come from the homeland of the Primeval Ones. We have come to inaugurate a new civilisation."

You hear yourself ask:

"What is the sense of life on earth? And what is the meaning of this temple?"

There is a movement and a rustling as they move closer to you, looking right into the very core of your soul. You feel their thoughts but cannot read their minds. Their semitranslucent reptile bodies shimmer and vibrate as they continue to transmit their thought patterns. They seem disturbed by your questions. Djehuty intercedes:

"This is the temple of Djeba, built for the great falcon Horus, Neter of spiritual self-transformation, and god of the Shemsu-Hor, Followers of Horus. The temple is dedicated to man's self-transformation when kingship was lowered from the heavens."

The temple continues forming around you! The fantastic display of building and manifestation of colour elevates you. The high exuberance of arrested movement and such richness of tones thrill you as the stories continue to unfold through incised lines on the temple walls, carved by invisible hands.

You are captivated by the magnificense of it all. It is the temple of Edfu! It is the temple of inward flame, of the secret soul of man.

For a brief moment, the walls are transparent and through them you see all of the Neters encircling the perimeter; their hands stretch forth, energising the very fabric of the walls that are fast turning back to a liquid gold in colour.

Your soul is lost in a dreamy magick; you are gone! But you cannot live in a dream forever. Such dreams are meant to be given the breath of life and then ushered into the world you inhabit. Free them!

Just in front of you is a doorway through which you see the river. Beside you stands a man whose lustrous green eyes gaze not upon you, but upon the waters of the Nile that sparkle with flecks of gold cascaded from the beams of the mighty Ra.

But this is no ordinary man; it is Horus, Neter of this temple. He stands tall; he has the perfect face of a determined warrior, not insensitive or cruel, but subtle, aristocratic, and refined. He wears a breastplate of fine white leather, scalelike in appearance, each segment edged with gold. His green and white pleated linen kilt too is edged with gold that makes tinkling sounds as a soft breeze moves around his legs.

Then you see what has taken his attention. A golden barque glides effortlessly upon the waters of the Nile, and carried on it is Horus's prize, his wife and goddess Het-Hert. Preparations for her journey have taken place at her Temple of Iunet two weeks before the new moon of Djehuty.

On board is the mayor of Iunet as well as members of Het-Hert's priesthood. Her state barque is being towed on the Nile upstream by a veritable flotilla of boats decked out in magnificent garlands of flowers.

By the time the goddess arrives at Djeba, it is late afternoon. She has made stops in several towns along the way, visiting sanctuaries of other deities, and has attracted an ever-growing company of followers from high-town officials, priesthood at other temples, and commoners and pilgrims of all walks and trades.

Horus now turns to you and says:

"Come, pilgrim, Het-Hert my wife awaits us on her state barque. We will prepare to go to meet the mayor of Abu."

Your excitement is hard to conceal as you walk side by side with the Neter Horus to board the waiting barque! On it you see the beauty of a woman, not an ordinary woman, but one bred of the Neters! Goddess of joy, goddess of love and loveliness. She radiates such serenity and dignity, it literally captures your breath and enfolds your being in a wave of pure, unconditional love. Truly her beauteous nature is worthy of a deep and unceasing love from her lord and mate, the mighty Horus.

Horus greets her with a sustained joy, almost typical from the completely thoroughbred person. Together they walk hand in hand towards a nearby shrine where the ritual of Opening of Mouth is conducted. Offerings of the first fruits of Ma'at are made before returning to the barque, whereupon they make a further stop at the Mound of Geb. Again the Opening of Mouth is performed along with other offerings.

Once ashore, Horus and Het-Hert proceed hand in hand into the outer court of the temple. They are accompanied by songs of welcome, sprinkling of purifying water, and burning of incense. They turn and smile at you before leaving via a side door that leads to the Mamissi. The only thing that remains is a heady aroma of patchouli, pine, jasmine, musk, and vanilla, which you breathe in deeply.

Djehuty is by your side, saying:

"They will spend tonight together to renew their sacred wedding vows. Then, after a further ritual, Het-Hert will go back to her temple in Iunet. But come, let us too celebrate their 'wedding night' and feast with the many."

Outside the temple grounds, pilgrims and townspeople are busy taking advantage of the free gifts of food and drink provided by the temples and visiting mayors and other high dignitaries.

Tables are laden with all kinds of bread and cakes; the smell of roasted oxen, glazed fowl, gazelle, oryx, and ibex reaches the sky.

Wine and beer flow freely throughout the town, as if the Tears of Isis have burst forth from the Two Caverns. Myrrh is being scattered on braziers; the heavy scent wafts up into the night sky.

Djehuty takes your hand as a group of merrymakers push their way towards the many dishes of food. Your guardian quickly piles some tasty morsels on a wooden platter and hands them to you:

"Feast and be merry, my heart's companion; we have much to sample on this sacred day."

You beam a wide and somewhat cheeky smile at your guardian; the joyous and ribald atmosphere is quite infectious. Down through the streets of the town you walk. Everywhere is bestrewn with faience, glittering with natron; the houses are garlanded with poppies, irises, and fresh herbs.

Youths too drunk to stand slump in doorways, shouting love calls to passing young maidens who blush and giggle. Rejoicing is all around and festivities are in all quarters.

"There will be no sleep to be had here until dawn," laughs Djehuty, grabbing a discarded wine skin and drinking heartily. Sleep gradually overcomes you as you lie down on a grassy verge, and close your eyes.

At dawn you awake with hopes and long to hear the songs of the dawn, but not so. On the morning of this second day at Djeba, you soon realise that it is no longer the beautiful reunion of god

and goddess, which was the focus of the previous night's cele-
brations. On this day, Horus and his wife Het-Hert are collected
from the Mamissi and are taken in great procession some distance
southwest, to the burial ground of Behdet.

The sky is a brilliant cobalt blue, but a greyness cloaks them
as they are followed in procession by a large number of priesthood, visiting dignitaries, and pilgrims. At the head of the procession, nine sacred lances are being carried.

Within a sacred grove of trees lay nine burial mounds of Behdet, in front of which are laid the lances.

"What are these mounds?" you whisper to Djehuty, who answers:

"They are where the children of Ra are buried, divine ancestors of Djeba. And see up there at the edge of this sacred grove."
He continues pointing, "It is the Upper Temple."

Whilst you wonder what these "divine ancestors" looked like,
priests say prayers, burn incense of kyphi, and pour libations
on the ground to the divine ones. Again Djehuty has read your
mind and, raising just one finger of his right hand, he causes the
ground to tremble and shake violently beneath your feet, sending
shock waves in the direction of the nine mounds.

Horus and his wife are unaffected by this and continue to
stand tall and proud whilst the priesthood and dignitaries around
them scatter; their chanting has now turned to screams of terror.

Each mound erupts like a volcano, sending earth, rock, and
sand flying into the upper reaches of the atmosphere. The once-
brilliant cobalt blue sky, without even the spectre of a cloud, has
been sucked away as an unhealthy darkness creeps across the
land. There is something oppressive here; an imprisoned feeling
comes over you.

You grab hold of Djehuty's left hand in fear. All is still. The
dust settles, and from beneath the earth rises the huge forms of
giants. Each being is seventy-five feet tall. Their shadows darken
all around you. Djehuty murmurs:

"Don't be afraid, pilgrim, they will not harm you. They are the nine children of Ra."

Their faces are kindly as they lumber towards you dressed only in a simple white loincloth. In turn each one bows low, his deep rumbling voice saying:

> "I am Ba-neb-Djedet—the ram who is Lord of Djedet where the soul of Wasir was worshipped as a ram."
> "I am Hor-Shefy—Horus the Ram-headed."
> "I am Menhi-Wer—the Great Butcher."
> "I am Hor-Shedet—Horus of Sheresy."
> "I am Neteraa-em-Sepetef—the Great God in his Province."
> "I am Neb-Shennu—the Lord of Trees."
> "I am Bennu—the Great Bennu Bird."
> "I am Henty-Bedhet—the One who is Preeminent in Behdet." ·
> "I am Neb-Hoot-Waret—the Lord of Hoot-Waret."

The nine giants now stand tall before you. They smile a smile that is both relief and sadness. From their enormous eyes tears fall, drenching the ground around you. Not even thinking of his height, you instinctively pick up the hem of your robe to wipe the eyes of the nearest giant. A warm glow lights his face and is transmitted to each brother, who in turn glows. No longer do you feel threatened but are gladdened by their presence and would like to be able to communicate further with them. But the mere movement upwards from their earthly tombs has weakened them and you can only look up at them smiling, but deep within, your heart aches. This is how it must be for these ancient beings, released for a brief period and then entombment until the cycle reaches its zenith once more.

Moments pass in silence as the nine children of Ra sway awkwardly; their giant forms are unused to standing for any length of time. Each turns away to tumble down into his respective mound, the earth, rock, and sand automatically covering them. Djehuty clears his throat, choking on his words:

"Their time on this plane will only ever be brief, as they must return to their sleep of sleeps for twelve of my moons."

No sooner have the ancestors been consumed back into their earthly tombs than the priests and dignitaries rush upon the graves, stamping and chanting madly.

Horror is written all over your face at their bizarre and in-sensitive act. Yet, you cannot help but laugh nervously at such outrage, and marvel at the effect of fear upon these people. Such ignorance! Djehuty touches your arm gently and explains:

"Like Wasir, they are kept buried in order to keep Khemit fer-tile for yet another year."

You perceive the figure of a child singing to the glory of Ra, or is it to the lost nine giants who rest in their earthly graves? You listen to the childish, trembling voice that sounds more like the twittering of a tiny bird. The air is now alive with music that has turned feverish; musicians arrive playing flutes, a merry noise of thin bright music backed by a clash of cymbals and now the beat of drums. The area soon fills with the joy of life. Now come the dancers! How supple they are; they seem to have no bones. Each one bending backward to the knees of the one who follows, one after another they come in line upon the mighty mounds.

Gaiety has now replaced solemnity. You walk away from the carnival-like atmosphere and turn your gaze towards the Great Temple of Horus.

"Edfu is the house divine of 'the Hidden One,' the perfect tem-ple of worship," you say to yourself. At that moment you feel as if all the worship of the world must be concentrated here and you are about to speak of this to your guardian.

But alas, he reminds you that it is time for you to go. In pious silence, you construct your pylons and walk through the portal to your world of familiar regions. Secretly, however, you yearn to return to Horus's halls to pray as those before you did when they entered the temples where strange beings were once worshipped. Utter your secret name to the gods and seal the door behind you.

FOUR

LEGEND OF SEKHMET

Thou art great of sorcery, cat of Ethiopia, daughter of Re, lady
of the uraeus; thou art Sekhmet, the great, lady of Ast.

LEYDON PAPYRUS

Sekhmet, whose name means "the Powerful One," is well known in her guise of lion goddess and enraged "Eye of Ra." She has been associated with other Neters such as Mut, Hathor, and Bastet, all with ancient origins but with very distinct personalities and energies.

She is the consort of Ptah in Men-nefer (Memphis), and was known as Mistress of Anktawy, "Life of the Two Lands," and mother to their child, Nefertum, god of the lotus blossom and perfume. They were known as the Memphite Triad.

In statuary, Sekhmet is usually shown with a leonine head and the body of a woman who is either seated, holding an ankh, or standing, holding a sceptre in the shape of a papyrus plant. Even carved in stone, this Neter exudes power and authority, with the ability to instill awe in the onlooker. During the reign of Amenhotep III, several hundred statues of the goddess were dedicated and placed in the precinct of Mut's temple in Thebes. Each statue was said to have a ritual purpose and was honoured on a particular day of the year. What a spectacular site they must have been when newly erected! Amenhotep III was known to have taken many of these statues of the goddess with him during his many battle campaigns.

To the inhabitants of Khemit, this Neter was a being that inspired fear as well as love, one which brought healing as well as sickness and death. In order to ward off the plagues her "messengers" brought at certain times of the year, spells were uttered and petitions made to the "lady of life" to keep all pestilence at bay.

She could heal as well as kill! In her healing guise, she had the power to mend bones. Her priests were renowned as physicians, surgeons, and exorcists, for only she could drive out the evil spirits who caused maladies.

Indeed, her epithet "Lady of the Bright Red Linen" gives an indication of the ferocity of this Neter's nature during times of conflict. As the Eye of Ra, Sekhmet watched over the divine ruler, both immortal and mortal, and kept safe the borders of her beloved land. Royalty embraced Sekhmet as protectress, calling upon her qualities of strength and invincibility in their battles with the enemies of Khemit, whom she laid waste with fire.

This "Lady of the Bright Red Linen" was well known for her bloodthirsty nature, which was displayed only when she meted out divine retribution. We are aware of the myth of Sekhmet inflicting carnage upon humankind as punishment for their duplicity and disrespectful attitude towards Ra. Brought to the edge of total annihilation, humankind was spared only because of the cunning of Djehuty and his ingenious plan to substitute red-dyed beer to lull the heart of the ravening beast and essentially make her drunk!

What is being presented here is neither new nor revelatory news. The pilgrim has to confront the Neter behind the many masks we have placed on her muzzle. Make no mistake, behind the veils and doorways of the inner worlds awaits this awesome power. She is one who will not be categorised, will not be subdued, will not be taken as an ideal for the "modern, emancipated" woman. Don't impose your modern values upon her, for she seems to have existed from a time beyond the known universe and sees no reason to change herself to satisfy our demands.

Sekhmet has been passionately loved by her devotees over the millennia and still continues to be revered by those of us who have not forgotten the Old Ones.

She must be approached with respect, NOT fear. Her radiant energies can burn our delicate neural pathways and the frail bodies we inhabit. Trial and tribulation can be the way of this initiatory path.

Think very carefully, pilgrim—what is it you want of Sekhmet? In fact, it might be best to ask, what it is that you ask of yourself?

PATH TO SEKHMET

Journey to Temple of Ptah and Sekhmet

Don your white robe and tie red and yellow cords around your waist. This will be in respect of the Neter you will be working with.

Build your pylons and make the sign of the ankh in the air above your head. On the lintel of the portal, hieroglyphs of Sekhmet appear:

Commit them to memory. This symbol is charged; look at each mark and take it within. As you utter your secret name, your journey takes you to the small temple of Sekhmet and Ptah within the great Temenos wall of Karnak Temple, where you will commune with the lion-headed goddess. This is a gateway that will take you to the heart of her realm. You will learn how to focus on her energy as you are drawn in.

Djehuty is standing in the shadows just inside the massive pylons of this great temple. There is a sense of urgency as he indicates that the god Ra is just about to rise. As he approaches, a rosy glow in the east sends a warm blush across the tops of the temple complex, which begins to stir into life. An ethereal garment now clothes the glory of mighty Ra. A cry wells up and you give voice to it. A hypnotic chant snakes its way through the desert, to finally nestle itself within the shadowed recesses of your mind. It is like a deeply resonant drumbeat, pulling you further and further into a vortex of energy deep within the temple.

Sekhmet, the Lady of Flame, knows you too well; she has released that which has slumbered through many lifetimes. No time to tarry now; Djehuty urges you onwards.

You enter Ptah's temple through seven gateways, most sacred of numbers, perfection itself. Each gateway is a doorway into three interconnecting sanctuaries dedicated to the Memphite Triad. A portico of two columns and a pylon precedes each sanctuary. Shafts of golden light, serving to heighten the atmosphere of deep sacredness and mystery, penetrate the incense-laden temple. Hieroglyphs and cartouches adorn each doorjamb. The walls are festooned with scenes of worship. Tuthmosis III, Shabaka, Ptolomy III, their names echo throughout the corridors, each one trying to outdo the other in homage to the Neters.

As you approach the first doorway, you notice something shimmering in the air, a whirlpool of energy. Uncertainty makes you hesitate but a voice whispers, "Let go of your fear; it is but a gateway into other states of being." In your heart you know the truth of that statement and step through. As you enter, you hear Djehuty's voice in your head and the words disturb you:

This small temple of Karnak holds a deeper secret. Once my statue stood here in this courtyard for countless summers as guardian to Ptah, Sekhmet's consort. But I was accused by the local peasants of being a genie of the temple and making Ptah my prisoner, and what's more, by copying and translating the few lines of hieroglyphs carved there, I had made

myself the master of the magick grimoire, which would com-
pel the surrender of the children-eaters. When my statue was
taken away, confidence was restored to the locals. But the
children continued to disappear.

Ah, too late to withdraw now! You find your guardian standing next to you, a wicked gleam in his eye but the very model of
propriety. Djehuty gives you a small pouch containing herbs and
saltpeter, explaining that you will use it as an invocation to the
god Ra. Before you have time to question this, he gently pushes
you through the doorway and into the gloom of a small temple
where before you stands the goddess Sekhmet in all her glory.

She is in statue form—made of pure red granite, forged within
the very heart of the sacred fire when the earth was cooling. Sunlight is filtering through a priest hole in the roof above, casting
a delicate beam directly on her. The statue of her is striking for
its slender body and narrow but curvaceous thighs in contrast
with her massive head that supports a flattened disk with raised
uraeus. She holds in her hands the wadj sceptre with the flowering lotus and the ankh of life.

A large brazier is before her. In it burns a blue flame. Instinct
tells you to cast the contents of the pouch into it. As it leaves the
palm of your hand, the flames rise and so too does your courage.
You stare into the now-blazing brazier, strength rushing through
you like crimson lava running through the earth's veins.

From within the core of the flame rises the great sun god.
Through the fire you see that Sekhmet is smiling; she is, after
all, the eye of Ra. You search feverishly for a form; you try to fit a
body to this mass of heat but each time it diffuses, carrying you
deeper and deeper into its fiery mass. In your mind's eye, you see
the form of the sun that is the life sustainer of this solar system.
It pulses with power, an unimaginably huge mass of energy. This
is a sentient being that has truly lived for "billions and billions
of years." Then you are given a glimpse deep into the interior of

your own planet, where molten lava flows through veins and fissures, bringing life, death, and renewal. A voice from within tells you to find your answer in the fire. But you do not know what to do. The flaming form of Ra frightens you; it is fear of the unknown.

Then the voice of Sekhmet booms out: "Feed your fears to the fire and nourish yourself with its heat." She commands, "Deliver yourself up to the flames."

You obey and feed the fire with all that has hindered you throughout life, blessing each problem as you cast it into the brazier, transmuting into higher energies as the flames consume them. The cleansing fire soon spreads throughout your energetic system, burning away the diseased and unbalanced parts until you are renewed and regenerated. The aroma of heliotrope wafts around you.

Your concentration is broken by the sound of soft singing that seems to be coming from within the walls, and you listen tentatively. The words sound familiar—where have you heard them before? Soon you sing with freedom and confidence with which the fire ritual has filled you. Your body begins swaying until the sound and rhythm has swollen to such force, you dance. Faster and faster you circle around the small temple, pushing beyond the first wave of exhaustion, accelerating past the shortness of breath. Beads of perspiration form on your forehead and gently trickle down your face. Your tongue is parched. You are no longer dancing but running instead. Where are your feet? All you can see are flames. Relentlessly you chant, now in gasps and raspy mutterings:

"My spirit has entered the flame,
Like the fire I am as bright as a star
I am Fire
I am Freedom
I am Courage

I rise through the living flames to the Neter
I am Resurrected."

A rush of energy hits you; your voice soars and now harmonises with the unseen chorus. The power is within you. From an unknown place, you hear your own voice now rise in pure joy. Finally the chanting drops to a delicate whisper; like a soft summer breeze in early morning it floats around the temple and then slowly fades into silence. You stop dancing and sink to your knees in front of the statue of the goddess who is now smiling upon you. Now the smell of heliotrope has taken on a different aroma that smells like light caramelized vanilla mingled with sandalwood.

The flames from the brazier have given way now to smoke that spirals upward through the priest hole, taking your prayers and wishes skyward.

You now stand proudly, shoulders squared, chin lifted with victorious pride. Sekhmet raises her wadj sceptre; the lotus flower is now a brilliant white emitting a delicate perfume that wafts around you.

"I am the Lady of the West. I look with pride upon one who has bravely faced me, the Eye of Ra. When you need me, touch your forehead and speak your secret name. I will hear you and aid you. Remain true to your heart and you will overcome adversity. Return now to your world of falsehoods and deceptions. Know that I am always with you."

You bow your head and turn to leave the temple. Your trusted guardian and friend Djehuty is standing in the doorway. A smile of mystery crosses his lips. You clasp his hand tightly as if to say, "I have survived and it feels good." Now visualize your pylons and walk through the portal to your world of familiar regions. Utter your secret name to the gods and seal the door behind you.

FIVE

LEGEND OF NUN

Your offering cake belongs to you,
Nun and Naunet who protects the gods,
Who guards the gods with your shadows.

PYRAMID TEXT 301

This path will lead you to the realm of Nun, when in the beginning there was only the swirling watery chaos, the "Primeval Waters." Nun is the name given to the state of being before the First Time.

The ancient Egyptians believed that before the world was created, there was a watery mass of dark, directionless chaos. Nun was the personification of the primeval waters, out of which was thought to exist both outside the universe and as part of every body of water from the River Nile to temple pools.

Nun was thought to play a part in the rituals involved in laying out the foundation for new temples, although he had none himself, nor any priesthood—and was never even worshipped as a god. Instead, he was epitomized at various temples by the lakes symbolising the chaotic waters before the First Time. In Karnak he was represented as the Sacred Lake and, at Abydos "Abdjw," by an underground water channel to what is now known as the Osireion.

But it was here in Karnak that the priests declared that Waset, Thebes, was the site of Nun's water and the rising of the primeval mound. Underneath this Nun lies inert, unending and indefinite, until Atum "rises" and "throws off" the waters to begin the act of creation. Nun is likened to "primordial soup" from which the Self-Created draws the necessary materials to create Its children.

It is said that eventually all things will return to Nun when they are completed; others say that Nun is a continual state of nonbeing enveloping the creations of Atum from which all new creations continue to manifest.

When personified, Nun is referred to as "the Father of Fathers and the Mother of Mothers."

On this path to Nun you will travel to the edge of chaos, where nothing makes sense but everything is possible, where miracles can happen. You will join the priests of old as they performed their daily rituals in the sacred pools dedicated to Nun, each waiting and hoping for transformation—a change in spiritual identity. Through this new identity you will venerate new values and beliefs.

Nun's form is emptiness, and the very emptiness is form. The same is true of feelings, perceptions, impulses, and your very consciousness as you bathe in the waters of Nun.

PATH TO NUN
Sacred Lake—Shi-Neter

Don your white robe and tie a blue cord around your waist. This will be in respect of the Neter you will be working with.

Build your pylons and make the sign of the ankh in the air above your head. On the lintel of the portal, hieroglyphs of Nun appear.

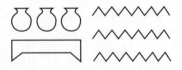

Commit them to memory. This symbol is charged. Look at each mark and take it within. As you utter your secret name, your journey takes you to the Sacred Lake of Karnak Temple where you will commune with the god Nun. This is a gateway that will take you to the heart of his realm. You will learn how to focus on his energy as you are drawn in.

A dawn mist is slowly rising from the waters and moves in lazy swirls around your feet as you make your way along a paved walkway towards the lake. You look around for Djehuty, but there is no sign of him so you sit on a stone bench and wait. The morning air is tinged with the promise of a glorious sunrise and more. Your eyes close as your thoughts enter the silence. Instead of hearing, you are *sensing* life around you. Vibrations move over your entire body, which has now become like a tuning fork, resonating deeply and strongly. It feels…good. An understatement if ever there was one!

The soft chatter of the priests who have now begun gathering round the sacred lake suddenly stops, causing you to open your eyes in curiosity. They are just standing at the top of the many stone steps leading into the lake, silently watching an ibis drinking from the waters. You are mystified by what is happening and decide to investigate. A young priest standing next to you senses that you are ignorant of the symbolism behind this act and explains that before they can enter the sacred lake, it has to be sanctified, and the only way this can happen is for an ibis to drink from it.

Ritual purity has always been important; everything and everyone who comes into the presence of the god has to be purified. Natron as well as incense and water for libations played an important part of the rituals. This would be followed by offerings to the gods. Since ancient times, they have bathed each morning in these waters before carrying out their temple duties.

As the bird finishes, it turns back into the form of Djehuty you have now become accustomed to seeing. But only you have seen this transformation from bird to god-form. Meanwhile the priests have begun their ablutions, uttering:

"Hear us, O Nun, the sky has not yet coming into being,
The earth has not yet come into being,
The gods have not yet been born,
And death has not yet come into being."

Djehuty beckons for you to come into the lake, and as you take the steps that lead down into the lake, the crystal clear liquid soothes and comforts your body.

There is a splashing around you as Amun, "the Great Cackler," in the form of a goose, takes flight, heading for the blue of the sky above. Then, as if a great weight is pulling you down, you gradually sink through these waters, no longer seeing the sky or the priesthood, just a nothingness, but it is not unpleasant. It doesn't even feel like water—you are now suspended, and before you is the core of central stillness feeling something emerging from within.

Huge dish-shaped mirrors appear around you, but it is not your reflection you see. It is the myriads of atoms evolving, and within each one is the primeval Logos, reflecting as the Great Eternal One. Then there follows a great silence. Impacting upon you is wave upon wave of frozen air as the Great Eternal One expels his hoary breath.

An ache becomes lodged within your throat and from the depths of your heart emerges a cry, a plea:

"O Eternal One! I have waited all my life to be taken to the very edge of the Universe and beyond, to see the eternal darkness, eternal chaos where the First Time is but a tiny spark within the emptiness of space. What are you, O Father of Fathers, Mother of Mothers? Does all begin and end with you?"

A voice replies:

"Many pilgrims like you have yearned to break free of your bonds to return once more to the Unmanifest and know who I AM! Then come, come with me!"

Try as you may, you cannot make out its form, but in your mind's eye you see and feel the climax of creating. As you reach the very edge of the beginning, you follow a trail along states of knowing and consciousness as the Great Eternal One reaches a further stage of knowing. You are then completely caught up in the creation as layer upon layer of formation folds in on itself, taking you with it. As it reaches a greater stage of knowing, layer upon layer of folds in action, layer upon layer, forming a new, ever-forming, aware of its knowing is the Supreme Logos in its being.

You are joyous, jubilant! Not even the deepest love or sadness can equal the intensity of knowing you are experiencing at this moment. Wave upon wave of vibration spirals out from the heart of the Being—may it never end! It increases in answer.

After a limitless time in motion, of great action and energising, there comes a time of greater stillness, there comes,

A Day of Manifestation.

You see an end created, out of which is born a new phase of coming into being, a coming forth of the grand order of matter. You hear yourself saying:

"From out of the One came all.
Complete in this order of being.
Complete in its coming into being.
Came the great laws of creation.
Thus emerged the First One.
Taught the great whirling motion,
Taught the stirring of the eternal,
And the organism of the Infinite within."

All is clear as you look up through the water unafraid, and you see Djehuty offering his hand to you. As he pulls you up and out of the Sacred Lake, you know that you have been on the edge of chaos where Nun came into being. You feel strangely purified and full of crystal coolness, where nothing makes sense and yet everything is possible and miracles *can* happen. But waiting for a miracle is rarely enough. Stepping into the water of being and transformation has somehow changed your identity. Djehuty looks deeply into your eyes, his searching gaze piercing layer upon layer of your Self to finally confront the truth within your innermost sanctuary. Satisfied, he lets go of your hand.

Your ordeal has made you quite sleepy. You lie down upon a stone bench beside the lake and, closing your eyes, you rest. The sun sets and the afterglow of Great Ra flames and fades. The clear, soft Egyptian night falls.

You are gently awakened by Djehuty who excitedly points to the Sacred Lake, where you see tiny lights glittering across the water, silvery white-like diamonds. But it is not the silver that calls you. Your imagination is held captive by the gold. You have been summoned by the gold! You cannot believe what is before you. Djehuty also marvels and tells you that the apparition you see is rare.

A golden barque has emerged from the waters of the lake, as resplendent as in the days of old, and the pharaoh who steers it is wrought in pure gold, and his sailors are of silver. As the moon shines, the prows of the barque leave a long wake of precious stones.

As the barque comes to one of the steps, you long to board this golden craft, but Djehuty stops you, saying:

"Those who climb aboard this phantom ship will return home laden with fabulous treasure, but everyone knows that if they make the slightest sound, even the merest sigh, the phantom barque, along with the golden pharaoh and the silver sailors, will sink immediately below the waveless waters of the lake and will engulf the foolhardy one forever. The appearances of the mysterious boat are becoming more and more rare, and one day it will disappear and will only be a memory."

You ask him why. He adds that it will not be seen again until there is no longer a liar, a cheat, a thief, and all those who transgress against one another throughout the world of man. Ah, such things are to be dreamt of; we the children of the gods are not without hope, though.

"There will come a day," Djehuty continues, "when the waters of Nun will inundate the whole world, and once again the universe will become the primordial waste of Nun's chaotic waters." You ponder on this and feel no fear, for you have bathed in the waters of chaos and emerged renewed. The mark of your becoming is the glyph for Nun, which is deeply imprinted upon your aura.

The priests have said their prayers to Amun, the patron Neter of Karnak, and have retired for the night. The "divine house" holds the sleeping god Amun, who will not be awakened until Ra has been expelled from the belly of Nut on the dawning of another day.

It is now time to leave the Sacred Lake and depart for your realm. As you rise from the bench you know that hidden beneath this vast and tranquil water is the unsettled and forever changing chaos of Nun.

Look upon the Sacred Lake in creation as a vessel, a chalice, and a grail cup to receive those mysterious energies. When you become the centre of these mysteries, then you are no longer human. You have become an awakened consciousness reflecting the whole of creation in yourself. Then you realize that consciousness, through you, is the source of creation.

Djehuty accompanies you as you make your way towards the Hypostyle Hall where you construct your pylons and walk through the portal to your world of familiar regions. Utter your secret name to the gods and seal the door behind you.

SIX

LEGEND OF KHONSU

I built a house for thy son, Khonsu in Thebes,
of good sandstone, red granite and black stone.
I overlaid its doorposts and doors with gold, and
inlayed figures of electrum like the horizon of Heaven.

HARRIS PAPYRUS

His magnificent temple can be found in the southwest corner of Karnak on the perimeter of the Temenos wall that surrounds the entire temple complex.

The Temple of Khonsu appears ordinary enough from the outside, until you cross the threshold. The symbolism of the moon is everywhere; a peristyle court bordered by a portico of twenty-eight columns divided into four groups and another with a grouping of twelve. The Hypostyle Hall leads into the Sanctuary of the Barque, in which chapels open to the left and right, and where to the east a staircase leads to the roof. It is not the roof that will beckon you to the Path to Khonsu, but the Temple of Opet via a warren of subterranean corridors and chambers.

This small temple is much more than a sanctuary for a god's worship. It became an integral part of the rituals and ceremonies surrounding Amun and the moon-child Khonsu.

The ancient Egyptians were at ease with the circumvolutions of the beyond. They had a taste for side exits, secret passages, concealed staircases, and the glow of phosphorescent tombs.

The name of the moon god, Khonsu, means to "cross over" or "traverse," related to "He who traverses the sky." In this path-working you will cross over the boundary to the other side.

Like the initiates of old, your path will originate in the sanctuary of his temple, and from the western darkness you will emerge into the eastern light of the Temple of Opet. This small Ptolemaic temple was built when Egypt was at its peak of initiation into the ancient mysteries.

It will be here that you will link with the elements of the soul beneath the dwelling of the moon-child.

According to legend, Mut and Amun's first son was Montu, but he was soon cast aside as he proved too fiery. When the goddess looked upon the face of Khonsu, she loved him immediately as he reminded her of the sacred lake in her temple, which is in the shape of a crescent moon.

From that moment on, Amun, Mut, and Khonsu were worshipped as a triad at Karnak and the Temple of Luxor.

As a lunar deity, Khonsu caused the crops to grow and ripen. Farmers sang hymns of praise to him for increasing their flocks and herds. He was also the Egyptian form of Cupid, who fired the hearts of the young with love. Those who prayed for offspring would consult the oracle of Khonsu to look with favour upon them. He also gave "the air of life" to the newly born. Khonsu, like the god of wind, Shu, was the lord of the atmosphere. He exercised control over the evil fiery spirits who caused the various diseases that took possession of human beings, rendering them epileptic or insane.

Khonsu was also known as the "giver of oracles" and his fame extended beyond the bounds of ancient Egypt. One of his popular names was "the Beautiful One at Rest." He was depicted like the Celtic love god Angus, "the ever young," as a handsome youth.

But, like the moon, Khonsu had a dark and hidden side to his nature, and was known as "the Hidden One." For this, his father sought him out to be the overseer of initiates who would seek their paths into the priesthood of Amun.

PATH TO KHONSU

Journey to Temple of Khonsu and Opet

Don your white robe and tie blue and black cords around your waist. This will be in respect of the Neter you will be working with.

Build your pylons and make the sign of the ankh in the air above your head. On the lintel of the portal, hieroglyphs of Khonsu appear.

Commit them to memory. These symbols are charged; look at each mark and take it within. As you utter your secret name, your journey takes you to the realm of Khonsu. This is a gateway that will take you to the heart of his realm. You will learn how to focus on his energy as you are drawn in.

It is a moonlit night and you are standing in front of the southwestern gate in the wavelike Temenos wall that surrounds Karnak. Ancient voices call out as you walk across paving stones, passing between a forest of pillars and a bank of sphinxes, all shrouded in darkness; you can just make out their ram's heads.

Then you hear a ruffle of feathers in the shadows and are relieved to see Djehuty as he transforms himself from bird into man. He greets you warmly, and together you walk through the portals of Khonsu's temple. All the while you are being watched over by even older deities that have been long ago etched into the sandstone walls around you.

Djehuty leads you onwards and upwards, crossing the vast, twenty-eight-columned Hypostyle Hall.

Darkness continues to cloak you; all you hear is your heart pounding within you. Djehuty realises that you are nervous in this gloom and, with a slight wave of his hand, wall sconces erupt into light.

You reach the outer limits of the Hall of the Barque, to the place of worship that belongs to the moon-child Khonsu, divine son of Amun and Mut.

Many internal voices ask questions. You hear more whispering phantoms from the shadows, all wanting to know your name and your reasons for entering this sanctum.

"What is your name, give us your name," cry the insistent voices from the darkness.

Don't forget—if you give your name, the forces will have power over you. Guard it for one you can trust.

But the voices persist, "Answer! What is your name, and why are you here?"

You still have time to run away back to your world but you carry on. Their screams have now turned to mutterings. "Hush now, he comes."

You just stand there trembling as silence greets you. Then the air is filled with mixed aromas of patchouli, gardenia, and cinnamon.

From the shadows of the pillars appears what looks like a statue of a man. His form glows in the faint light of the wall sconces that gently flicker through the darkness. At night Khonsu reigns quietly over the plains of Karnak, and the wind harbours whispering phantoms retelling the story of his magickal powers.

You are riveted to the spot as Khonsu stands before you, not as a statue, but a living god. Even in the gloom of the temple you can see how truly handsome he is. He is a young man in the posture of a mummy; he wears a close-fitted dark blue cap with the royal side lock, the antet, protruding out of one side. On his young chin is attached the punt beard. Above his head a moon disk gives off a pulsating opalescent glow.

In his delicate hands he holds the triple sceptre—crook, djed, and flail—that gleams with an inner life. His voice is youthful and boyish as he speaks:

"My fellow god Djehuty was indeed very wise to bring you here. Many have attempted the journey along this initiatory path. Some reached the morning of the east, whilst others stay forever in the darkness of the west." He smiles as he finishes the last sentence.

You look for your guardian but he has changed himself once more into an ibis and stands in a corner, busily preening his feathers.

From that moment on, you are in the hands of Khonsu and follow him as he glides on a stream of air across the threshold of the Hypostyle Hall and into the inner shrine.

Centred in this room is placed an altar, stark and empty. You stand there as the initiate, at the beginning of a journey but you have no idea what you are in for. With all your might, you summon up Djehuty, who is suddenly there by your side, and taking your two hands he places them on the altar of sacrifice. There is reassurance in his eyes that tells you that you will not be alone.

The contact of the cold stone on your hands makes you flinch, then a surge of energy pulses through your body as velvety darkness turns to light then back again, awakening the mystery within your being.

Khonsu utters words that are completely alien to you, but the strange sound they make soothes and quells your fears. He then instructs you to walk around the altar anti-sunrise seven times, and as you do, all memories of a past life are unlocked. These will help strengthen you throughout your initiatory experience.

Imagine that your life is a ball of wool slowly being unravelled as your present life experiences fade into the background. You begin to feel lighter as burdens are being lifted from your shoulders. Each step is the turning of an ankh in an ancient lock to a chamber that guards your past memory. Some of these memories may not be easy to face, but you overcame your adversities and survived. Drink deep from that well of strength within you and look only forward.

There is a surge of pressure at the back of your skull that feels as if it will burst. You hear a voice, but this time it is Djehuty who speaks:

"Many other pilgrims before you have sought the same entry into the ancient mystery school, but have failed in their quest. It is going to be a difficult road to travel, but the rewards are great. At times you will feel alone and abandoned; it is all part of your re-member-ing. In spirit, I will always be with you. Now return to the altar and place your hands upon it."

You obey his command and find that your hands rest in an indentation in the stone and your fingertips are pressed firmly into it. On the far wall, a large slab of stone begins to move smoothly across the floor, revealing a darkened entrance leading down to subterranean caverns. You pause to take deep breaths; each one is in tempo to a drumbeat. Like a mantra, sound waves swirl around you that hold you in a trancelike state, and in this state Djehuty guides you through the portal that leads down into darkness. Before you enter, he says:

"Know this, that only in darkness can you unlock your old memory and awaken your dormant sleeping brain to relearn the secret rites of mystery. These were once practiced in the ancient caverns of these subterranean chambers that were all out of limits to the mundane creatures of the world. Only those seeking entry into the ancient mysteries can gain entry. Go now, find the ankh that will open the door."

Down the many steps you stumble. Each one is of doubting and melancholy; sadness becomes your companion. You are being stripped of worn-out values and standards. You feel your outer shell dissolving. It is painful, as if being flayed alive and then salt added to the wounds to reinforce the suffering.

Corridors of darkness greet you, and a pungent smell of incense wafts round you, but it is not sweet; it is acrid and foul-smelling and stings your eyes, nose, and throat.

In this murky swirl, you stop and listen. There are sounds of footsteps, but are they walking forwards or backwards? Now confusion is your companion, brought here to bewitch you with its power. A shrieking voice threatens:

"I shall drive you back with much dishonour, O seeker of the inner mysteries, right back to your land of greed and ignorance, back to your spiritual darkness and ignorance!"

You twist and turn to face the direction of the voice that now laughs at you.

"Get back to your creature comforts. You have no business here!" it shouts in your left ear, making you jump.

But you do not listen as you have come here to face your demons and prove your worth amongst your ancient priesthood.

More silence surrounds you as you move slowly forwards along a neverending corridor. Then an eerie green light is emitted from crypt and cavern that beckons you to enter. There are seven in all, and you visit each one in turn. All are womblike in construction and each contains a phantom whose screams echo around the walls, sending you reeling back into the corridor.

You cry out in the gloom and cup your hands over your ears to shield yourself against the voices that are beginning to make you feel lightheaded, causing your body to drift in a vacuum.

Swirls of a different kind of ether move about you as Shu, lord of the airy realm, whips up his forces. Sylphs begin preying on your very being, their wispy fingers lifting you until you feel featherlight. Your body now drifts through airy currents whilst their thin sweet voices sing to you:

"We are the binders of life, the very breath that breathed life to live. We are the carriers of the ancient seeds of being to the planets, and unto the ends of the universes. We are the vital spirit, moving and forever changing, that which dreams are made of."

As the Sylphs come nearer, you see an ankh being passed amongst them, but each time you reach out to take it, it fades away, lost to you. You are left with the sensation of old and out-dated memories being sucked out as new life is breathed in. You hear yourself saying:

"I will never have that ankh."

As suddenly as the Sylphs appeared, they vanish, sucked into a great vortex of flames. Out through a wall of fire strides the shining being of Sekhmet-Montu, the falcon-headed one. His golden eyes fix you with a steady gaze and from his heated nostrils sparks and flares shoot out, licking your airy body.

Flames continue to stream outwards from his huge form that only serve to fire your senses, breathing even more new life into your being. As he extends his fingers towards you, fire creatures of all shapes, colours, and sizes encircle you, licking you with their greedy fiery tongues. The overall feeling is incredible.

"Who are you?" you scream in terror.

"We are the Salamanders, spiritual beings that inhabit the element of fire, and through us, fire exists. We are the strongest and most powerful of all the elementals, having the ability to extend or diminish our size as needed. We and others of our kind are mischievous spirits. We are like children who don't fully understand the results of our actions, as such, and it is up to you to use strong control over us when you use us to aid your magick."

You become totally fascinated by these small lizard-like flames that begin to weave a web of golden fire of gossamer-like strands about your shoulders that culminate in a glorious cloak of splendid firelight. As you are bathed and encircled into the realm of Sekhmet-Montu, you hear yourself crying out:

"May this rapture be neverending!"

Again you are being tantalised by the glimpse of the first ankh held in the fiery grip of this god.

Then, without warning, water swirls about your fiery body, sending steam hissing and spitting about you, dissolving your glorious cloak into vapour. This is the realm of Hapy.

As the waters rise about you, you swim in all directions whilst the dual forces of the god Hapy flow below you in his murky depths. Deep into his watery realm you are tugged until you meet the spirits from his domain. They are beautiful, and you become completely dazzled by them as they swim around you, their watery fingers grabbing at you, pulling you farther under. To and fro you are tossed as these playful creatures coil their watery forms around your overburdened body. You are completely under their rule. You ask again:

"Who are you?"

"We are the Undines, who control the forces of nature in relation to plant and marine life, as well as the tides and motions of water. You will find us in rivers and lakes and in the far seas and oceans of your planet. You will also find us in the vapor of the air you breathe, but you must take care of us as we have strong influence over your emotional well-being, as everything that lives and breathes contains the element of water."

Deeper and deeper they pull you, as if you are a mere plaything. You can feel the last of the air leaving your lungs as you go down. Then, above you, you see the ankh floating and you grab it for dear life, forgetting all. At last you struggle free from the Undines' watery clutches and escape, rising to the surface, gasping for breath.

From this watery mass and firmly holding the ankh of life, you climb onto the ancient mound of the Ben-en-et, over which was built the small Opet Temple.

You sit on the dry earth mound within this temple, completely exhausted, and think about your ordeal; you have been frightened by the airy creatures of Shu, singed and burnt by Salamanders of Sekhmet-Montu, then plunged into blue-black liquid by the forces of Hapy. You passed through all the elemental forces of your first initiation and feel cleansed. You now understand why so many initiates have perished before you, but you have emerged triumphant with the ankh that unlocks the door to the world beyond.

You so much want to tell Djehuty about the many obstacles that presented themselves in the underground crypts, and how you have emerged triumphant with the ankh! And there he waits to greet you as you are bathed in the golden glow of Ra as he comes forth from Nut in the east.

Djehuty looks into your eyes and sees a change within you. Again you have entered into another Neter's realm in perfect love and perfect trust. You must ask yourself, what have you learned? The elements have touched you and in their own way spoken to you.

You have trod the path of the many initiates before you—reflect upon this as you leave the Temple of Opet.

Djehuty is there by your side, smiling as you construct your pylons and walk through the portal to your world of familiar regions. Utter your secret name to the gods and seal the door behind you.

SEVEN

LEGEND OF AMUN

The Temple is the House of God.
The Body of Man is the House of God,
Therefore the Temple is the Body of Man.

R. A. SCHWALLER DE LUBICZ

How true the above text is when we work with the Neter Amun in "Ipetresyt," the Temple of Luxor. The god Amun was always an enigma because he represented absolute holiness, and in this respect, he was different from any other Egyptian Neter. In the eyes of the ancients, Amun remained independent of the created universe. He was concealed and invisible like the wind and thus was associated with the air as an invisible force, which facilitated his development as a supreme deity.

Amun was looked upon as the Egyptian creator deity par excellence and, according to Egyptian legend, was self-created. The ancients believed that he could renew himself by becoming a snake and shedding his skin. But at the same time, Amun remained apart from creation, completely different and independent from it. But his temple represented the true embodiment of man in God's image.

Although Amun is associated with the principal complex of Karnak, his main temple of worship and function is in the sanctuary of the Temple of Luxor.

The great scholar Schwaller de Lubicz spent fifteen years of onsite research at this temple. From the very beginning, he knew it was special and measured everything from blocks to inscriptions, proving that the plan of the temple was originally based upon the human form. Furthermore, it was designed symbolically to represent man.

He found the square root of five commanding the proportions of the Holy of Holies, the inner sanctuary of this temple. Many of the ancient Egyptian edifices were directly built and incorporated the number five into their very structures. The Egyptians also made extensive use of the Golden Section, which commands the flow of numbers up to the number five. Indeed, the human body is divided by the rule of the Golden Section, exactly at the navel. The Temple of Luxor is divided into five sections.

It is within this temple that, together with this Neter, you will experience the opening of your five senses. Five is the key to the vitality of the universe, its creative nature. Five terms are required to account for the principle of creation; five is accordingly the number of potentiality. Like the Neter Amun, potentiality exists outside time. Five is therefore the number of eternity and of the principle of everlasting creation and eternity. Ironically, the fifth letter in the Hebrew alphabet is "heh." Coincidentally, the hieroglyph "heh" is a pictogram of a man raising his arms in prayer and signifies "eternity."

This path like no other will impact upon your senses. It will awaken you to the inevitable rebirth of the sacred essence of man that has involved itself in matter. Amun in his temple is a symbolism of primal energy.

PATH TO AMUN

Journey to Luxor Temple

Don your white robe and tie a blue cord around your waist. This will be in respect of the Neter you will be working with.

Build your pylons and make the sign of the ankh in the air above your head. On the lintel of the portal, hieroglyphs of Amun appear.

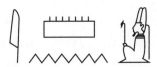

Commit them to memory. This symbol is charged; look at each mark and take it within. As you utter your secret name, your journey takes you to the Temple of Luxor where you will commune with the god Amun. This is a gateway that will take you to the heart of his realm. You will learn how to focus on his energy as you are drawn in.

The scene that greets you on the other side is a magnificent avenue of sphinxes with ram's heads that seem to be forever watching the all-changing world around them. Beyond them is the great Temple of Luxor. It is so perfectly formed that for a moment you don't even notice Djehuty standing there in front of you, busily making notes on his palette with his stylus. He smiles his knowing smile and together you walk the short distance to the House of Amun.

Two great obelisks born of granite loom upwards, rooted in the earth and pointing significantly skyward, joining earth to heaven.

You marvel at them and ask Djehuty what they mean.

"These are Pharaoh's votive offering to the Neters. The top of each obelisk, like the pyramids, are all representations of Ra's first light on the newly born earth."

They seem to be murmuring a message to you that makes your ears burn! Then the murmur becomes a piercing cry of a bird, so loud you have to cup your hands over your ears. Djehuty senses that you have felt the inner meaning of these totems to the Neters, but tells you that this will be revealed in another path farther along the River Hapy.

The cry has now turned to an echo, but you can still feel it within your head. Eventually you shift your attention to mammoth stone figures that straddle either side of the huge pylon entrance; they seem unafraid of their loneliness. A voice behind you speaks:

"These are of my father." Turning around, you meet the gaze of a tall man, his face dignified. Piercing, fathomless green eyes scrutinise you but they are not unfriendly. He is dressed in a fine white linen kilt. Over his left shoulder hangs the leopard skin worn only by the Sem Priest, order of the god Set. In his right hand he firmly grasps the uwas sceptre of office. His perfume-oiled body glistens in the sunshine, his smile is radiant. He is Prince Khaemwaset, son of Rameses II.

"Ipetresyt awaits your entry. This holy temple was designed and built by the first Amunhotep and has been added to by many other Pharaohs to become a masterpiece of man in God's image."

You look at him curiously, not knowing what he means. Around you the colours on the walls dance before your eyes; the temple lives! This temple holds a spell. As soon as you enter it, you feel the touch of the lotus as if an invisible hand has swept a blossom lightly across your face; the perfume is sublime and makes you swoon with pleasure. Ancient memories rise up from the depths of your heart; they knock at the doors of your conscious self, yearning for release. The intensity of your emotions at this moment cannot be fully expressed!

With each step you take with Khaemwaset, a tide of energy surges through your body. Pausing for a moment, you can hear the voices to the old gods, sounds of music, words of wonder. The prince beckons to you to follow deeper into the Neter's house towards the sacred sanctum, total centre of man's being.

The colours become richer; you are now completely at one with your surroundings. A lector priest of prayer and cleansing prepares to make Prince Khaemwaset pure before approaching the sanctum. He washes his mouth and face with natron. You are invited to follow suit.

Temple singers enter, shaking sistra and gently swaying. They sing notes warm and welcome that serve to awaken Amun, "the Hidden One," from his slumber.

The prince now prostrates himself on the marble floor, rises slowly, and bows before the doorway, then breaks the red clay seal before entering the sanctum of the great Neter.

Passing behind the veil into the inner chamber of the sanctuary, the Holy of Holies, with trembling lips and downcast eyes, the prince calls upon the Neter.

All is dark within. Lamps are lit beside the statue of the great and golden body of the god.

Amun stands there before you, in human form. He gives off a beautiful aroma of jasmine, lavender, and pine. On his head is a deep circlet of gold from which rise two straight parallel plumes. His chest is bare and begins to rise and fall with each shallow intake of breath as censers are waved through the air, now filling the shrine with more heavenly fragrance. All inhale the fumes of kyphi that waft freely around the temple. You feel euphoric as the air you inhale and exhale is breathing life into the statue of the great god Amun, whose eyes now begin to open. You have the strangest sensation of looking out onto the world through the god's eyes. The energy within you is rising to its highest mortal point and is beginning to merge with very essence of the divine.

Taking up some fine mist-linen that has been dipped in scented water, the prince touches the perfect body of the Neter, washing him slowly and in silence. As the liquid is applied, you feel the sensation of being touched and cleansed, to finally stand in a state of flawless purity.

With much reverence Amun is fed with fine foods. The sensation of taste in your mouth is sublime, each mouthful an exquisite melange of flavours.

Then Amun is clothed again in fresh raiment. You feel the wonderful sensation of the freshest, purest, white linen against your skin; it encloses you within its soft embrace, almost like pure light raining over your form. How can this be? What is this temple doing to you?

As the god closes his eyes, you are once again in the sanctuary watching as the prince steps away from Amun. He raises both hands upward slowly and utters up a prayer to the Neter:

"O mighty force of earth and heaven
That quickened waters of all chaos,
Breathe sacred life here unto Amun.
O mighty power of earth and heaven
The Great Spirit, Divine Creator,
Impart to me your words of wisdom
So I may once again be mighty.
O Great Cackler, O great Amun
Who sprang forth from times primeval
As an egg, Akasha symbol
Made all things come into being
Spread your bounty over Waset."

You stand there in awed silence, watching this royal prince of Khemit in devotion. After several more libations, you both leave the sanctum, closing and sealing the door in silence. But an inner voice whispers to you:

"I, coming forth, am Amun—the Hidden One—pure of heart within the pure body. I live through my words."

You stand outside the holy shrine listening, waiting, and watching, looking with two eyes of wonder, eyes that always seem to be asking a question. Djehuty joins you as the prince takes his leave.

"Let us walk now through the temple. This is the structure of your body. Divine is this temple structure; feel the surging of the power!"

But is it power? Or just enchantment? Do you feel different in your body? Djehuty touches your arm gently, saying:

"We have put you to trial. It is the retuning of your body that you sense. The entire structure of this temple has been shaped and fashioned using a system of numbers through geometry and symbol, all pure forms of man's connection with the macrocosm above. The sacred number of all being has once again entered your body."

It is true what he has said to you. Even the very censing, cleansing, opening of the eyes, feeding, and playing of music to Amun has served to open your five senses to all that is around you.

"Let us now leave this hallowed place together."

The once-bright colours on the pale brown sandstone wall and columns have turned almost yellow in the sunshine. The aura given off is delicate and soothing and calms your beating heart. The deep reliefs upon the stone soften the walls and you pass right through them and back into your own form.

You are not the same person who first walked into the great Temple of Luxor. You have been in the presence of "the Hidden One," where you engaged in prayer with a Sem Priest. Holy rituals were enacted. Your soul, your great Ka, merged into your being. Deity entered your body in wondrous transformation and made you pure.

As you look deep into Djehuty's eyes, the reflection you see is that of the temple itself. You are in there as it is there within you. He reaches out and touches your forehead, saying:

"Whenever you have desire to return to the temple within, touch your forehead thus."

You thank him for showing you the way and turn to leave, but something makes you look back, just one more look at this incredible temple; but when you turn around, the vision you see is yourself. You *are* the temple. Now construct your pylons and walk through the portal to your world of familiar regions. Utter your secret name to the gods and seal the door behind you.

EIGHT

LEGEND OF ANPU

*The Great God looketh upon thee, and he leadeth thee along the path
of happiness. Sepulchral meals are bestowed upon thee,
and he overthroweth for thee thine enemies.*

PAPYRUS OF NEBS

Anpu was an ancient funerary deity who was manifest in numerous guises and took many appellations, but essentially remained the great god of the dead and lord of judgment in the afterlife. Or not, dependent upon which priesthood was in power!

His worship was widespread throughout Egypt from an early period, but his major cult centres were based in Abt, Zawty (Assuit), and Hardai (Cynopolis).

Anpu usually took the form of a black jackal and is referred to in some texts as Sab, but he was always a dark canine inhabiting the desert fringes and burial sites.

At other times, the Neter took human form but with the head of a jackal, which was worn as a mask by his priesthood during the funerary rites symbolising the presence of the Neter, especially during the Opening of Mouth Ceremony.

Over time, Anpu's ascendant star in the heavens was overshadowed by the prominence of Osiris and eventually his attributes assimilated by him. Anpu was then gathered into the Osirian family as the offspring of Nephthys and Osiris.

The Neter's many epithets give an indication of his most important duties as guardian of the dead. As Khentamenthes' "Foremost of the Westerners," he held authority over the dead in cemeteries, most of which were on the West Bank of the Nile.

Originally Khentamenthes was an older canine deity whose cult centre was at Abydos. In his guise of Tepy-dju-ef, "He who is upon his mountain," he watched over the dead and kept hostile forces at bay from a vantage point overlooking the burial grounds. As Khenty-she-netjer, the one "presiding over the god's pavilion," he took charge over the embalming tent and secure burial chamber, which in the case of royalty was known as the "Golden Hall."

Anpu's association with mummification was recognised during the Pyramid Age and his epithet of Imy-ut, "He who is in the place of embalming," emphasises the importance of his role in the process, especially in the preservation of the king's body from decomposition. The Imy-ut was also a fetish associated with the Neter; it took the form of a headless animal skin, usually a feline, which was tied to a pole stuck into a pot. It was Anpu who was said to have taken charge of the embalming of Osiris.

As with certain of his brethren, Anpu's image and mythology have become blurred and buried beneath fabrication and retelling. We must use more than physical sight to see beyond into the shadows to find the Golden One shrouded within the velvety darkness of night and the starless skies. The great god of the dead waits impassively and patiently for us to learn well the lessons of life before we enter the Hall of Judgment to face the ultimate, the judging of our heart.

It is interesting to note that during the conversion of the ancient Egyptians to the Coptic religion, they took the image of Anpu with them, giving him the new role of "Protector of Travellers Abroad."

As Christianity in Egypt took its hold, this Neter underwent yet another change. His dog head was replaced with a human guise and he was renamed Christopher, patron saint of travellers.

Whatever his guise may be, Anpu continues to remain with us to this day, as our protector in life and death. With this in mind, pilgrim, let us proceed to the place of Judgment within the Temple of Amun in ancient Djamet (Medinet Habu).

PATH TO ANPU

Journey to Medinet Habu

Don your white robe and tie brown and black cords around your waist. This will be in respect of the Neter you will be working with.

Build your pylons and make the sign of the ankh in the air above your head. On the lintel of the portal, hieroglyphs of Anpu will appear.

Commit them to memory. This symbol is charged; look at each mark and take it within. As you utter your secret name, your journey takes you to the West Bank of the Nile where you will commune with the god Anpu. This is a gateway that will take you to the heart of his realm. You will learn how to focus on his energy as you are drawn in.

You emerge into a twilight world. It is silent, remote, vast, and mysterious. The scent of evaporating heat hits your nostrils, intermingled with that of aromatic herbs. You stand for a while just drinking it in.

Then the air about you becomes very still, unnaturally so, which makes you slightly nervous. You wonder where your guide is. Suddenly the touch of a hand on your elbow makes you jump.

Djehuty's smiling eyes twinkle down at you. You take his hand and walk towards a great temple that looms out of the dusk. In ancient times it was known as Djamet.

"Why have you brought me here?" you ask him. He looks at you shrewdly then answers in measured tones:

"Is this not the moment you have been waiting for, even asking for? When you, the pilgrim, seek answers, pulses from your heart reach me, and I answer."

Fear and uncertainty rise up from your solar plexus, making you stumble, and you tighten the grip on your guardian's hand. You hear an inner voice within, saying:

"It is too soon, too soon."

"Too soon, too soon!" mocks the wind. Even nature mocks your fears! Phosphorescent stars light up the velvety darkness. Djehuty scans the surroundings quickly and urges you onwards.

You approach the main entrance to the temple via pylon gates. Sheer polished walls tower majestically towards the night sky. Four flag poles are contained within niches in the walls; their flags flutter strangely in a now-windless night. Your guide seems a little perturbed, which is a little worrying.

"I am only concerned that we reach the place of Judgment on time. You must commune with your Heart before we begin."

With that, Djehuty places a jewelled heart scarab in your hand. You look at him with surprise and then understanding dawns. So it begins…

Passing through the pylon gates and turning to the right, you walk towards a small temple, the Temple of Anpu, which stands upon the holiest of sites, a primeval hill emerged from the waters of Chaos in a time even before the gods existed. There are several steps to navigate before you come upon enormous bejewelled doors, which open silently, admitting you both. A priest and priestess wait patiently within the portal; they take positions on either side of you whilst your guardian follows behind.

You are taken to a tiny side chamber, dark except for a small brazier and two oil lamps. The scent of incense drifts towards you, sweet and spicy; it stimulates long-lost memories. A wooden beaker containing wine is handed to you and you are encouraged to drink.

"It will soothe the hurts and wounds which may rise from the depths of your heart."

You tighten the grip around the heart scarab that nestles safely in your left hand, then you drift off into a deep sleep.

You find yourself walking along a long corridor, dimly lit by torches, the smell of sandalwood and frankincense incense weaving between the pillars, becoming ever stronger as you reach a doorway at the end of this neverending corridor. Protective hieroglyphs are deeply etched all round the lintel; as you commit them to memory the scarab in your hand starts to pulse. This does not disturb you, rather it serves only to reassure. You go through the doorway to be met by a priestess, robed in gold and black. Her features are finely sculpted, with a full mouth and deep, dark eyes. She watches you intently, then a smile breaks the solemnity of her gaze.

"You are exactly how I imagined you to be, a little nervous, but that will pass."

You wonder who she is and before you can utter the question she answers: "I am the guardian of that most sacred temple you call your heart. You have served the god within well, have no worries on that account. I have guarded this holy place from before you entered this world, nurtured it, loved it, and birthed it."

Her words make you catch your breath and tears well up in your eyes. She continues:

"To be true to your heart is more precious to you than any riches this world or the next could offer."

The priestess looks at you and nods her head. Yes, perhaps now is the time to express that which has remained hidden within this most precious temple. You want to say so much, then you hear yourself utter:

"I present myself, stripped bare of any artifice, embellishments, and subterfuges. It has been a life less than perfect, filled with pain, disappointment, and regret. My pride has caused me to fall many times and my anger extinguished many a hope. Compassion and mercy have flown to the winds on many occasions and wisdom buried beneath the sands. I have not heeded the words of those who are wiser than myself and, like a headstrong child, have stumbled on obstacles of my making. Yet, hope drives me on, for:

"Without memory of my beloved Khemit
I should be nothing.
Without love of my most beloved Neters
I should be nothing.
Without humanity
I should be nothing.

"My heart has felt much which has been dark but the glorious light of Ra has shone within its recesses, illuminating its beauty, joy, and grace. This much I have offered others. Will you accept me as I am?"

The heart scarab begins to pulsate rhythmically, and with each pulse you feel a ripple of energy flow outwards from your own heart. The very heart of the known and unknown is contained within yourself and it is a doorway you feel compelled to go through. Dare you take that leap of faith? You focus the energy in your heart centre, using it as a key. Then you feel a surge move through your body.

After what seems like aeons, a hand on your shoulder gently brings the present into focus. It is time to enter the chamber of judgment—the Weighing of the Heart begins. Figures line the walls on either side; only their outlines are visible, the rest is lost in shadow. Not so! A group of figures wait at the other end of the chamber; majesty and power emanate from them, bathed in golden light, they are set apart from all which is of the mundane world. They watch silently and without expression. You are beckoned to come forward, only to find the chamber has dissolved and stars surround you on all sides. Djehuty moves into view, scroll and stylus ready in hand. Ma'at stands to one side and as you look beyond them, Anpu sits majestically upon a golden throne. Your heart leaps within your breast at the dog god's magnificence. He was ancient when Osiris swept into the land of Khemit, "Lord of the Hallowed Land" and "Foremost of the Westerners." Impassive eyes scrutinise with thoroughness; there is nowhere to hide. He is resplendent in obsidian blackness, strongly sculpted jackal head, broad shoulders, sweeping down to muscular hips draped with a gold kilt, and as always the uwas sceptre. He is sheer power and authority, not to be trifled with.

Ammut the Devourer lurks oppressively in the gloom, too awful to face, yet inescapable. There is no movement for what seems like an eternity, then you are asked to place the heart scarab on the scale. Ma'at takes the feather out of her headdress and places it on the other side.

Djehuty's measured tones ring out, "The time has come to account for your life. Be open, be truthful. Seek neither to prevaricate nor fabricate. We know all and we see all. Begin."

The scroll of your life unravels, bit by bit. The hieroglyphs burn on the surface of the papyrus, glowing with intensity, and they are now on fire! A whole lifetime is encapsulated in this one moment. The words flow onwards, manifesting in almost-forgotten scenes, some uplifting, and others unbearable in their clarity. Such was earthly life, a myriad of transformative experiences.

Out of the corner of your eye, you glimpse Djehuty's stylus continuing to fly across the papyrus, ceaselessly recording every utterance. Will you be declared "true of voice"? Then it ceases and all eyes focus upon the gigantic scales that are now traced out by stars in the expanse of the heavens.

The delicate balancing of the scales must not be hurried. The vibration of your heartbeats echoes loudly, deep and sonorous, hypnotic in their rhythm.

A pronouncement is made and, whether acceptable or not, it is for you, and only you, to judge. It will have great bearing on the life which is to come. This has *not* been a judgment but an initiation of the most profound kind.

Mighty Anpu steps down from his throne and approaches you. The earth shakes with each step he takes. Banish all preconceptions you have of this ancient Neter; he is son to no one, no mere psychopomp but Great Initiator, Lord of the Underworld. He gestures for your heart to be returned to you. A tightly bound papyrus is also handed to you—the contents of which are known only to you. He speaks and you listen:

"Remember that life is a series of what you may call challenges, but these are not in continuous motion. There have to be periods of quiet reflection. Time to think, breathe, and feel, and to understand how far you have travelled on this, *your* journey. Life begins with reason, it has purpose, but the greatest shame is that you forget these reasons almost as soon as you are born. For life on earth, which is so full of the complex issues of survival, causes us not to remember that there is indeed purpose behind the chaos I call life. However, as you are aware, from chaos comes order. There is purpose and there are opportunities for you to grow or stay in what I call a state of neediness. Life is full of many materialistic views and therefore occupies your mind more than the spiritual pathways you should be taking. When the time is right, change will occur. Take my blessings and prosper well."

It is time to take leave of this sacred space and return to your own time and place. To linger too long in the realm of the dead is to bring many calamities upon yourself. Djehuty appears by your side as the stars fade and the solid walls of the chamber take shape once more. What have you learned? Have you understood what Anpu has said to you? Will it change your perception of what existence and consciousness actually are?

Soon the temple doors loom into view and you are ushered into the already bright dawn. The morning air is ripe with dew and the glorious face of Ra is steadily rising in the skies. You bid your guide farewell until the next encounter.

Utter your secret name to the gods, go through the portal into your world, and seal the door behind you.

NINE

LEGEND OF MERETSEGER

We have the confession of Neferabu, a modest employee
at the necropolis, who admits to having been justly stricken
with illness for his sins. Afterwards he proclaims that he
has been cured by the goddess "Peak of the West" (Meretseger),
having first repented and ardently besought her forgiveness.

PAUL HAMLYN, *EGYPTIAN MYTHOLOGY*

Meretseger was portrayed as a coiled snake with the torso of a woman, even as a cobra-headed woman. Her name means "She Who Loves Silence."

Meretseger was the goddess of the famous necropolis outside of Waset and was believed to have lived in a pyramid-shaped mountain that rose a thousand feet above the Valley of the Kings. In ancient times, the mountain was named after her, "Dehenet Imentet," which means "Peak of the West." This also connected her with the peak in the Egyptian mind, making them one.

Other deities were generally not fixed to a specific geographical location. They may have been worshipped mainly in one town, but were not the personification of that place. Whereas, Meretseger became the personification of the peak; she did not move, so any who revered her *had* to be near the peak.

During the New Kingdom, Meretseger was the chief deity over the Valley of the Kings. For the tomb builders living in their village, in a valley behind the hill of Ta Set Ma'at, Meretseger was a danger-ous Neter who spat poison at anyone who tried to vandalise or rob the royal tombs. She was also the patron deity of the many workers who built these tombs, and punished those workers who committed crimes, but healed those who repented.

Sin was not part of the ancient Egyptian mindset. They fol-lowed Ma'at and any deviation from this was deemed chaos, rather than sin. None of the other protective or vengeful deities had such an unusual impact on the thought pattern of the eve-ryday Egyptian as did this one goddess. She was a goddess who protected and healed those who admitted their sins and asked for mercy. Her followers would invoke her, naming their wrongdo-ings, asking the goddess for forgiveness. Such was the power she had over them.

But there came a time when work ceased in the workmen's vil-lage as royals and nobles chose to bury the dead in other areas of Egypt, thus her worship faded.

This path will give you an insight into Meretseger's powers of protection when the tomb of Prince Nefrekeptah is robbed by a royal prince who is intent on owning the legendary Scroll of Dje-huty. Great feats of magick will be demonstrated.

PATH TO MERETSEGER
Journey to the Valley of the Kings

Don your white robe and tie brown and red cords around your waist. This will be in respect of the Neter you will be working with.

Build your pylons and make the sign of the ankh in the air above your head. On the lintel of the portal, hieroglyphs of Meret-seger appear.

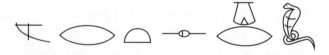

Commit them to memory. This symbol is charged; look at each mark and take it within. As you utter your secret name, your journey takes you to the gateway that will take you to the heart of Meretseger's realm. You will learn how to focus on her energy as you are drawn in.

Your ever-faithful guardian Djehuty is waiting for you near a village in a sheltered valley behind the hill of Ta Set Ma'at, "Place of Truth." This is where the workmen who create the royal and private tombs in the Valley of the Kings and the Valley of the Queens live with their families.

It is a fascinating place and you want to stay and walk through the streets and look into the houses, but Djehuty is anxious to reach the cavern where the goddess Meretseger presides, as she has sent him word of trouble in one of the tombs and, as she is the guardian of the City of the Dead, it is she who must keep the order on this side of the River Hapy.

At the southern end of the workmen's village, you rush with your guardian along a dusty, well-worn narrow path that leads over Ta Set Ma'at to the west. At the top of this hill, the path forks in two directions where Djehuty veers off to the right down another path that slopes gently downwards towards the Queens' Valley. Tucked neatly in a shallow cavern is the shrine to the cobra goddess, but it is empty! Djehuty is muttering to himself and is very agitated. He is behaving so oddly, he begins to lose his shape, resuming his ibis head, then switches back again.

"We have to go to the place of the dead but we have no time to walk. Take my hand." Within no time at all you are transported into the realms of the dead and are standing in the burial chamber of Prince Nefrekeptah. There's an eerie glow within the chamber that turns everything a pale green. You hear voices coming from a corridor outside the chamber, and as they get closer you can detect that they are the voices of two youths. One is clearly very anxious.

"Calm down, it's only bats. They live here on the walls of the tombs," one of the youths says. But the sound of his voice only excites more of these nocturnal creatures into flight. You can hear the flapping of their leatherlike wings as they collide with the youths.

"Put out the lantern!" the dominant youth commands. Darkness cloaks them like a shroud making the other youth moan with fear.

"Be brave, brother. We must be very close to the burial chamber. Let us wait here for a while then we'll light our lantern."

"No need, brother, look! There's a light just ahead of us. You can relax; we have reached the burial chamber of our ancestor."

You can now see clearly the two youths standing just a little distance from the doorway of the chamber. One seems older than the other, but it is clear that they are related as they both have similar features. Both wear heavy dark blue cloaks. You try to stand behind Djehuty, but he assures you that you and he are invisible to them.

"Aren't you coming in?" he asks his younger brother.

But the youth just stands outside the doorway, holding the lantern and shaking with fear. He points to the lintel above the entrance of the chamber.

Carved black basalt guardian sculptures stand on either side of the entrance.

"Brother, look! There are carved images of Nefrekeptah struggling to free a scroll from its watery tomb at the bottom of the River Hapy! Please, brother, I beg you, don't go inside the chamber. First look at these scenes; they are truly awful! There are great serpents surrounding him. Please don't enter this fearful place." The youth pleads, reading more.

"The next scene depicts him reading from the scroll. It is written that this did not please the god Djehuty, so he decided to take vengeance on Nefrekeptah for saying the sacred spells and gain-ing the ultimate magick powers. The next scene is really tragic as it depicts the drowning of his wife Ahwere and son Merib."

But the youth's words go unnoticed and the older brother steps through the doorway, into the burial chamber, and stands gaping at the magnificence of it all.

Jewel-encrusted thrones, leopard skins, and ivory caskets filled with precious gems dazzle him. Djehuty tells you that this wealth accompanies the dead to their afterlife.

In the midst of this treasure stands an immense stone sarcophagus containing the mummy of Prince Nefrekeptah.

Then the youth's attention is drawn to a small table at the foot of the sarcophagus where a strange light is being emitted, casting a gentle glow throughout the chamber. Within this glow lies a papyrus scroll. The youth knows instinctively that he is looking at the Scroll of Djehuty. Silence is all around him as he makes his way towards it.

"This is easier than I thought," he says as he reaches down to pick up the papyrus. But a sudden movement in the chamber makes him stop. Floating above the sarcophagus of the dead nobleman is an apparition of a coiled cobra with a woman's head. She is both beauty and deformity and holds the youth in her gaze. He is momentarily frozen with fear. You cling onto Djehuty in fear as the creature hisses:

"I am Meretsssssseger, guardian of the West Bank. Prince Sssssetne, why do you come here to disturb the sleep of the dead?"

"How do you know my name? I have not been here before," he gasps in surprise, recoiling back in fear. Meretseger drops to the floor of the tomb and begins slithering towards him.

"I know all by name who come here to try and steal our prize. You had better leave if you want to live another of Ra's days."

You stand fascinated, watching the scene unfold before your eyes. Djehuty is next to you with his arms folded over his chest; there is a broad smile on his face. Meretseger is aware of your presence but chooses to ignore you.

The goddess edges closer, scratching the skin on the prince's legs with her scaly body. She hisses continuously at him, licking his face with her forked tongue; a heavy aroma of honey, clove, and cinnamon wafts around the chamber. Never has he been so scared, but he plucks up courage and says in a small voice:

"Yes, it is true I come for the Scroll of Djehuty. I need the magick it contains."

"Sssssetne, I must warn you that it is not ordinary magick. It contains the most powerful spells of all time, and not one magickian has ever used it wisely, especially a puny young prince such as you." She screams in laughter, sending echoes around the chamber.

"I am fifteen summers and I am a trained Sem Priest to my father the pharaoh."' Setne retorts angrily at Meretseger who is now lashing her tail on the floor of the tomb, causing puffs of dust to rise up around them, making the prince cough.

"If you take this Scroll of Djehuty, it will bring you nothing but despair and disaster, especially with one so young as you. Do you want your life cut short like that of Prince Nefrekeptah?" she spits, whacking her tail against the stone sarcophagus.

"I may be young but I will use it wisely. I, I solemnly promise you that, I, I do learn quickly," he stammers. "I am *also* a magickian."

"A magickian indeed! It is not enough for a magickian to learn the practices of the scroll; he has also to learn how to keep the secrets safe. In the wrong hands it will prove catastrophic for the owner." She says, continuing to hover over him. Her warning does not put him off; it only makes him more determined to have it.

"I promise that I will not share the magick with another mortal soul," he says, edging towards the table. But the goddess slides quickly down, preventing him from getting any closer.

"Sssssetne, you do not understand the power of the scroll." Meretseger continues. "Djehuty, the god of wisdom, wrote this with his own hand!"

"Then with such power I can do much for Khemit," the prince says.

"This scroll has brought much misery to the previous owner, who lies in the eternal rest of the dead. He also had great plans for Khemit." The mistress of Dehenet Imentet warns.

"Your brother Anhure has more sense than you," she says, pointing to the younger prince, who remains cowering in the corridor.

But the impetuous prince will have none of it and makes a grab for the scroll. At that very moment, Meretseger is joined by the ghost of Prince Nefrekeptah himself, who is not as accommodating as the cobra goddess.

"The Scroll of Djehuty can never be yours!" The chilling voice booms from behind its glittering golden mask.

"It has cost me, and the lives of my precious family, and almost brought the downfall of the land of Khemit."

Setne, although shaken at the sight of this latest apparition, continues, saying:

"Let me have the scroll or I'll take it by force!"

"Setne if, after hearing all I have told you, you will take no warning, then the Scroll of Djehuty must be yours."

With that, the prince makes a grab for it. But the dead Prince Nefrekeptah reaches out, grasping Setne's wrist with his icy hand, saying:

"But first you must win it from me, by playing a game of draughts. Dare you do this?"

"Just a game of draughts? That's easy enough."

"Don't do it, Setne, it's sure to be a trick," warns Anhure from the corridor.

Setne ignores his brother and calmly seats himself on a couch near the ebony and ivory draughts board.

"Prince Nefrekeptah, I am ready to play."

Setne and Prince Nefrekeptah begin their first game, but the dead prince moves the silver and gold pieces about the board with just the power of his mind. This does not upset Setne, as he turns out to be a skillful player. That annoys the dead prince, who murmurs a spell that wins him the first game.

"That's cheating!" protests Setne, only to find the ground of the tomb opening up, causing him to sink into the floor up to his ankles.

You are disturbed by this scene and wonder why Djehuty is allowing this, but the Neter reads your mind and replies:

"I want to have some fun with this young royal."

His younger brother tries to rush in to help him, but is barred entry to the chamber by an invisible force that sends him rocketing backwards along the passage, leaving him helpless.

Without a word the board reassembles the pieces and the second game commences. Setne loses that too. All the while, with the aid of Djehuty, the dead prince keeps uttering spell after spell, sinking his partner deeper into the ground, this time up to his waist. Although Setne is scared, he still refuses to admit defeat and signals for the third game, staking his life against the Scroll of Djehuty.

Silence again reigns as the board refills itself. For the third time, Setne loses as another spell is uttered, opening the ground further to swallow him up to his chin. With a cry of utter desperation and panic, he calls to his younger brother:

"Anhure, give me the amulets of Ptah and the spells of magick! Hurry—I'm choking!"

Already a spell is being uttered that sends Setne further into the ground. It is no longer a game to win but to save his life!

As Prince Nefrekeptah makes his winning move, forgetting his fear, Anhure runs into the chamber and places the amulets of Ptah against his brother's head, then begins uttering the spells of magick. Instantly Setne feels a surge of power that frees him from the dead prince's enchantment, forcing his body upwards out of the earth of the tomb. Setne then extends his hand and makes a grab for the Scroll of Djehuty, immediately plunging the burial chamber into total darkness.

"Run for your life," he yells to his younger brother, who has been transfixed by the entire episode.

The two princes dash from the chamber, along the long passage, and through the labyrinth of rooms and false corridors away from the screams of the dead prince.

"You have taken away the light and now I will be in eternal darkness. I beseech you, prince, bring back the scroll, bring it back so that I may have the light," Prince Nefrekeptah pleads.

"He'll be back!" Meretseger hisses furiously. "And he'll need more than the amulets of Ptah to protect him next time!"

You leave the darkness of the tomb with the screams of Prince Nefrekeptah echoing in your head, and are aware of Meretseger slithering past you, disappearing along the corridor in pursuit of the two princes.

You are stunned and confused and cannot fathom why Djehuty has allowed the scroll he actually wrote to be stolen by two young princes. But he smiles, reassuring you that what the young princes stole was just a roll of papyrus.

But you are sure that you saw magickal symbols on it.

"Ah," he explains, "these symbols are for my eyes only, or for one who is pure enough to read these signs and not use them for their own purpose. Look deep within your heart and ask yourself if you are that person."

Djehuty tells you that it is time for you to leave the realm of Meretseger. Construct your pylons and walk through the portal to your world of familiar regions. Utter your secret name to the gods and seal the door behind you.

TEN

LEGEND OF SET

The king is my eldest son who split open my womb,
He is my beloved, with whom I am well pleased.

RECITATION BY NUT, THE GREATLY BENEFICENT

He is known by many names—Sutekh, Shaitan, Setekh, to name a few—but we commonly know him as Set.

Naqada is supposedly where he was born. It is said that the goddess Nut loomed above the housetops of this town, dripping starlight. It must have been like the explosion of a supernova when Set, the star-child, burst out of her side and fell to earth.

The ancient town of Naqada lies on the West Bank of the River Nile (Hapy), downstream from Waset, modern-day Luxor. Traders in those days had easy access to the Red Sea coast and the gold reserves of the eastern desert via the Wadi Hammamat. Naqada and Koptos on the opposite bank were naturally placed to be the centres of the predynastic gold trade.

In those days the ancient world revolved around gold. Not only did the possession and control of this precious metal ensure earthly power, it was as essential to their mysteries as crystals are to many of the New Age movements today.

Naqada was the necropolis of the town of Nubty, known in Greek as Ombos. Gold was mined here. Gold was of the earth and of the sun; it was torn from the darkest caverns of the world, and nothing shone like it. It was obvious to everyone that the mines belonged to Set, Set of Nubty as he is called in the Pyramid Texts.

Gold had real magick within it and everyone knew that too. Gold was holy, gold was fertile. In those ancient days, parents would often place small-bagged portions of their native earth beneath the birthing beds of their children, then imagine the effect that gold might have upon a special son.

This particular place was a real melting pot and a crossroads where peoples from all over the known world gathered either to share new innovative ideas, or continue with their own particular primitive lifestyle. This cross-section of citizens varied not only in ethnic groupings, but also in social strata.

Set has become a controversial figure in recent historical researches and discussion, but all the facts are not being disclosed. Scholars have attempted to strip him of his reputation for originality and genius, harmony and pure brotherly love, by maintaining that his chaotic actions universally were something to be highlighted and condemned. They have called attention to his murderous ways and continued alienation of all things harmonious.

Whoever delves into the fathomless secrets of the land of Khemit, or is held captive by the fascination of the five millennia of history before the Christian era, cannot help but admire the great kings of ancient Egypt who worshipped and fought under the name of Set and continued to bring both fame and fortune to this black land.

PATH TO SET
Journey to Naqada

Don your white robe and tie black and red cords around your waist. These will be in respect of the Neter you will be working with.

Build your pylons and make the sign of the ankh in the air above your head. On the lintel of the portal, hieroglyphs of Set will appear:

Commit them to memory. This symbol is charged; look at each mark and take it within. As you utter your secret name, your journey takes you to Naqada, first capital of Khemit, and birthplace of a boy child to the star goddess, Nut. This is a gateway that will take you to the heart of his realm. You will learn how to focus on his energy as you are drawn in.

There is desert all around you and the mild wind has whipped up sand sprites that leave a fine film of dust over your robe and a gritty sensation in your mouth. This is after all Set's country, which will reveal to you more of the mystery surrounding the son of Nut.

Walking toward you is your guide Djehuty, who greets you with a beaming smile. You would like very much to talk to him, but feel a little shy and awkward. He reads your mind and just raises a finger in the air.

For the moment nothing visible remains here in Naqada, but nevertheless the clues are everywhere, pointing to a crossroads of peoples and the meeting of minds:

"It was here that the first invaders from the seas came to establish a higher kingdom. With them they brought new customs, and a new religion." Djehuty says. "Now close your eyes, then slowly open them."

You do as he says and before you is a walled town of brick connected to a series of cemeteries. There are over two thousand graves packed into seventeen acres overlooking the River Hapy.

As you walk through these ancient places for the dead, you see that graves have been placed side by side, virtually saturating the area with tombs.

"Everyone wanted to be buried in Nubty: they wanted to leave this world as gods under the same influences that Set had felt when he entered it," Djehuty remarks.

Just in front of you, a group of men and women have gathered. All are crying bitterly and covering their faces with the dust of the ground. Edging closer, you see that a pit has been prepared for the body of a young girl. She was as beautiful in life as she is in death. Wildflowers have been woven into her red-brown hair.

The girl is lovingly and gently placed on a reed mat in the pit in a contracted, fetal position, reclining on her left side with legs flexed and arms bent, hands in front of her face. Her head lies at the southern end with her face pointing to the west.

Little ornaments of shell, some bright stone beads along with a handmade-polished red-ware jar, baked clay figurines, amulets, and carved ivory plaques are placed around the dead girl. These will go with her to the afterlife.

The women's crying has now turned to a mellow chant as the men place a ceiling of interwoven branches and brush over the pit, followed by a covering of earth.

One by one the women come forward and place a pebble on the grave for each summer of the girl's short life—twelve in all.

As you continue to gaze down into the earth, Djehuty has walked farther up onto the ridge and is now calling you to join him.

He extends his hand down and helps you climb to the top. Slowly, out of the horizon appears a red granite temple built on a monumental scale. It shimmers in the rays of Ra. You stand there spellbound, just drinking in the beauty of this awesome structure.

You just have to clamour down from the ridge and on to a stone-paved road that leads you to a huge carved doorway dominating the entrance to the temple built for the god Set. But as you approach the entrance, a cosmic darkness surrounds you, a tender darkness beyond, a darkness that is consecrated. To feel this darkness is more wonderful than triumph, and at the end of it is love.

Far above you shines the evening star of Khemit, watched over by the star Alcor in Ursa Major. So wonderful is this heavenly sight it stirs the very core of your heart, and from it is released a song so pure that it awakens the very soul in the heavens.

Within this starry mass is the blessed Nut, suspended in the infinite starlight. You become absorbed in the stars about you, and are at one with the stellar dust of the goddess. All around you the cosmos is flushed with purple and then crimson as Nut's blood reddens the stars around her radiant body.

Then, in the moonlight and starlight, between electric storms that rage through the heavens, pain grips the stardust body, and bursting out from her bright side comes the firstborn of her children. Set! You rejoice with the goddess as she works her magick birthing her baby.

You hear her proclaim:

"He is my eldest one, born of darkness from starlight, my child of wonder." She whispers the message of dawning:

"I am the primeval goddess, stellar mother bringing onward the seven star souls; I bring forth my star-child Set." Thus cries the star one to her baby:

"O my son, my true beloved, Son of Evening, God of Dawning!"

So is born the child of wonder, the first male-child Set, first Neter of the black land. Down he falls beneath the stardust, passing silently through the twilight, from the stellar to the firma, down he drops to Nubty.

All have gathered now to witness the birth of this being and, as you stand there in awestruck silence, the Son of Evening descends.

He is the son of tenderness and passion. You can see the fire in his bosom, and the beauty in his spirit. You see the mystery of his being, a dual side to his delicate nature, a duality that will split into two beings—to form his twin brother Heru! His mother cries her last song:

"Golden child, and dearest Sutekh, I give to Nubty precious gold ore, for gold is of pure kingship. This gold will make all kings holy, but as they tear it from the darkness of the earth-world, it will echo the time when you were torn from my bright side through the cosmic darkness, and so, my dear one and only star-child, each time they rape the gold from the earth, you will be reborn."

You close your eyes and imprint this scene in your memory and inwardly make a wish. The aroma of cinnamon, sandalwood, amber, and lemon is all around you. The scent is wonderful! Dje-huty gently taps your left shoulder and you open your eyes to a vision standing before you of pure angelic wonder. It is Set. His golden body shimmers in the darkness of his sanctuary. Red-gold curls frame his perfect face that holds an expression of all-know-ing, understanding, and perfect love for all who look upon him. His bright green eyes look beyond all space and time and hold a hint of sadness of things yet to come; the future that waits is one filled with deception, brutality, and loss. Yet, it is inescapable and his destiny.

Resting on his golden shoulders is a fabulous malachite collar edged in the curious animal body form he will always be likened to. On the breastplate are golden hieroglyphic symbols that you can read and he mouths:

"I am he who came into being
And in coming into being
Created the beings who came into being."

You hear the splendour in his speaking as words melt from his fine mouth. Like the shamans of old, he sings songs from distant ages taken from the stellar waters, music from the whole of creation.

He is clothed in a leopard skin that is the mark of his beloved mother Nut. Each spot represents a star on her glorious body. From henceforth, shamans, priests, and the infantry will drape this skin across their shoulders. In future times they will forget the reason why they wear it. But embedded deep within their psyche, they know they wear it as the shamans of old—a mark of respect for and in recognition of Set.

You long to be able to reach out and touch him, but he raises his left hand and a circle of black flame surrounds him. Djehuty whispers to you that the time is not right. You then try to connect with him on a different plane. This time it is the inner voice of Set that responds, promising that he will meet with you again as you journey through the land of Khemit. He smiles a smile like warm sunshine falling on cold stone.

But behind his eyes, his young face has a deep pathos. His silence bids you be silent, and his stillness bids you be still. And his sad and absolute acceptance sifts awe, like the desert wind which sifts sand into the temples, and into the temple of your heart. A great silence envelops this temple; vast and unknowable, it shrouds everything in a velvety darkness emanating from the dawn of time. Such sorrow flows out from its heart!

And you feel the touch of time, and the touch of eternity too. In this magnificent sanctuary, he whispers:

"I will be with you always."

This warmth touches you deeply as you are led away by Djehuty.

All are joyous in Naqada as they look at Set "Har-Iu," their ever-coming son, and claim him as their greatest offspring. In his honour they build around him this monumental temple hewn out of the finest red granite. They wave banners of gold, red, and yellow and with them you chant to their god of Nubty:

"Set is great, Set is master,
Let us honour him in splendour,
Let us gather beneath these rafters,
In his shrine renowned and ancient,
Let us sing the song of Sutekh,
Burn the sweet incense of kyphi,
Make libations of beer from barley,
Make libations to the star god."

While the people of Nubty sing, a falcon is steadily rising in the air and circles around Set's temple. You see that this is an omen, as the falcon represents Horus.

Now you see a time of confusion when from lands far across the sea to Khemit come longhaired invaders from Sumer. By the thousands they come in their high-prow boats, ready to conquer the simple folk of the Naqada valley.

You watch in horror as the invaders smash the skulls of the inhabitants of Nubty with pear-shaped maces made of the precious dark blue lapis lazuli stone.

From these people of Sumer will spring the sacred kings and elite families that will always remain part of a special blood clan calling themselves by the grand name of Shemsu-Hor, Followers of Horus.

They will carry their standards into battle supporting the kings who bear the title of Horus, "May his name echo forth forever."

Those from Naqada, who choose to stay, live apart from these usurpers and are known as the Companions of Set.

It was at this time in the First Dynasty that Narmer, also known as the Scorpion King, commenced the digging of an irrigation canal, gradually fighting off the desert and the old ways of life of his people.

Gradually the communities draw together in increasingly large units and eventually form the Two Lands—the northern kingdom is ruled by the darkling earth-god Set, whilst in the south is his bright sky-god twin Horus, arched over by the Great Mother Nut.

Grassy hills and fields replace the sand dunes, and the old life gives way to one of rich and plenty. You watch and listen as all the peoples sing together:

"We are one! We are a nation!
May all our kings be known as Horus!
May their names live on forever!
Let us unite the twins of Nu'it,
Let us call them Sutekh-Heru,
Form Two Lands of ancient Khemit."

Narmer was great indeed, you think as you continue to watch the saga unfold before your eyes. It was Narmer who brought together two warring brothers and made them face one another, giving them each a crown: white for Horus and red for Set, symbols of upper and lower Khemit. Together all pharaohs unto eternity would wear these two crowns.

You look up at the now-blue sky and know that you have travelled on the astral plane to the wondrous stellar realm of Nut.

You ask yourself, what you have learned from these visions? Like the left and right sides of the human brain, like the higher self and the lower, Narmer allowed twin powers in the form of Set and Horus to coexist together. You smile at Djehuty standing beside you, and he gives you a reassuring smile back.

As you leave the place where Set was born, everything around you dissolves back into the desert sand, leaving just the wind sprites for company. You have seen so much that has disturbed you. It is a truth you have not been aware of.

Visualise your great pylon in front of you and walk through its portal to your world of familiar regions. Utter your secret name to the gods, and seal the door behind you. Set the star-child greeted you; as a stellar miracle you shall remember him.

ELEVEN

LEGEND OF HATHOR

O thou beautiful Being, thou dost renew thyself in thy season in the form of the Disk, within thy mother Hathor.

PAPYRUS OF NEKHT

Hathor was known as Het-Hert and Hetheru, Athyr, Lady of Malachite, and Lady of Turquoise. Her worship originated in predynastic times (fourth millennium BC).

She was the matron and embodiment of what were considered the pleasures of life five thousand years ago, and which for many continue so to this very day: joy, love, romance, fertility, dance, music, alcohol, and perfume.

Although she was inherently connected to the female of the species, Hathor cannot be considered only a women's deity as she also had a large and devoted following among men.

As she was associated with metal, she held spiritual dominion over the Sinai Peninsula, and was responsible for the success and well-being of the mines in that area. Hathor was intensely worshipped by male miners and soldiers, as she was by women in childbirth or young girls wishing for husbands. Both genders readily recognized the sacred divine within her seductively vibrant, joyous beauty.

The name Hathor means "Hut of Horus," but it may not be her original name. The link with Horus can be traced back to the Narmer Palette, where Hathor is depicted at the top of the famous palette overseeing the events detailed therein. In the centre of the palette is Narmer wearing the white crown of Upper Egypt, whose symbol is the flowering lotus. To the right of the king is kneeling a prisoner, who is about to be struck by the king. Above the prisoner is a falcon, representing Horus, perched above a set of papyrus flowers, the symbol of Lower Egypt.

Since that time, Hathor's principal form was that of the cow, and was strongly associated with motherhood. At the temple of Queen Nefertari at Abu Simbal, the queen is depicted as Hathor on many of the wall reliefs, and in another sanctuary Rameses II, her husband, is shown receiving milk from Hathor the cow.

When a child was born in ancient Egypt, seven Hathors (somewhat like fairy godmothers) would appear to "speak with one mouth," and decide the child's destiny.

Hathor's own child was Ihy, who was worshipped in Denderah with her and Horus-Behdety. Like his mother, Ihy was a god of music and dancing, and was always depicted as a child bearing a sistrum.

Hathor, the female companion of Apis the Bull, was often pictured as a naked lady, having horns and holding the sun on her head. Like Sekhmet, Hathor was closely connected with the sun god Ra of Heliopolis, whose "eye" or daughter she was said to have been.

In her cult centre at Denderah in Upper Egypt, she was worshipped with Horus. At Dehr el-Bahri, in the necropolis of Thebes, she became "Lady of the West" and patroness of the region of the dead.

Her other title, "Lady to the Limit," means in every sense "limit" to the edges of the known universe, and "Lady of the West " is a perfect devotional title in her funerary stance behind Osiris, welcoming the dead to their new home.

She is also associated with numerous other Egyptian goddesses and has also been absorbed into the many characteristics of Bat, another predynastic cow goddess (as depicted at the top of the Narmer Palette).

Occasionally she may appear fierce and terrible, but she is *never* unattractive. Her imagery too is unlimited. It is interesting to note that Hathor habitually takes more forms than perhaps any other ancient Egyptian deity, most of whom are limited to one or two shapes. In terms of imagery, she is possibly the most fluid of all, matched only by the notorious god Set.

Her connections with the fiery temperament of Sekhmet are softened when associated with Bastet.

The cult of Hathor is unusual; whereas most other Neters have priests of the same gender, both men and women were Hathor's priests. Many of them were artisans, musicians, and dancers who turned their talents into creating rituals that were nothing short of works of theatrical art. Music and dance were part of the worship of Hathor like no other deity in Egypt. Hathor herself was the incarnation of dance. Stories were told of how Hathor danced before Ra to cheer him up when he was in despair.

Around 400 BCE, Plato shared this profound belief:

"Music is a moral law. It gives soul to the universe, wings to the mind, flight to the imagination, a charm to sadness, gaiety and life to everything. It is the essence of order, and leads to all that is good, just, and beautiful, of which it is the invisible, but nevertheless dazzling, passionate and eternal form."

PATH TO HATHOR

Journey to Denderah Temple (Temple of Iunet)

Don your white robe and tie a yellow cord around your waist. This will be in respect of the Neter you will be working with.

Build your pylons and make the sign of the ankh in the air above your head. On the lintel of the portal, hieroglyphs of Hathor will appear:

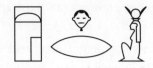

Commit them to memory. This symbol is charged; look at each mark and take it within. As you utter your secret name, your journey takes you to Denderah Temple. This is a gateway that will take you to the heart of Hathor's realm. You will learn how to focus on her energy as you are drawn in.

A sensation of pure joy overtakes you as you approach the magnificence of White Denderah. It stands in solitude upon a blackened mound. From far off you see the façade, large, bare, and sober, rising, in a nakedness as complete as that of Isis rising from the Nile, out of a plain of brown, alluvial soil that is broken only by palm trees that contrast sharply with the white walls of the temple, their fronds throwing a feathery embrace across the earth. The silhouette of a lone hawk breaks the expanse of endless blue skies. The great Horus keeps watch over his lady.

You look around for your guardian Djehuty but he is nowhere to be seen. The walls around you soften and you feel a current of energy pulsating from within. This temple holds you spellbound as soon as you enter, and again you feel the touch of the lotus. It is as if an invisible and kindly hand has swept a blossom lightly across your face and down towards your singing heart.

The years drop away from you, as do all cares and concerns, and you sense that every golden hour will bring another drop of wondrous essence that sets time at defiance and charms sad thoughts away. This is a special place indeed.

You enter the temple, and stand awestruck in the first hall. It is mighty, magnificent, and full of enormous columns from which faces of Hathor look down to the four points of the compass.

The brightly decorated walls around you are proof of the builders' and artisans' love and devotion to their goddess as they hailed and worshipped her, with the purity of white and the

sweet gaiety of turquoise. The depth of such emotion has sanctified the very ground the temple stands upon.

You look up again at her face; it is a delicate oval shape. From
under a perfect brow, slanted green eyes gaze down at you. Her
full lips smile protectively upon you. You reach out to touch the
column, and as you extend your hand you feel a stirring behind
you, and hear the faint jingling of temple sistra! You turn around,
and standing before you in the entrance to the second hall is a
statuesque woman, perfumed and clothed in a diaphanous robe of
white, blue, and orange. The air around her is a mix of jasmine,
musk, vanilla, and patchouli. Her warm smile envelops you totally
as does the welcome in her eyes. In her left hand she holds a bronze
mirror, and in her right a sistrum, which she shakes gently.

"So beautiful to behold," you murmur to yourself. Her kohl-
darkened green eyes sparkle, skin of olive, and hair as black as a
night sky. It is the goddess Hathor who speaks:

"I am Mistress of Iunet, bountiful mother. My breasts have
suckled gods and kings. I am the wild cow of the rushes whose
dance excites all living things. I am the fiery power of the Wadjet
that spreads terror of the king through all the land.

"I am part of the first great culture to infuse its entire society
with the magick of music and dance. My people have enjoyed life
to its fullest, and no celebration in Khemit would have been complete without music and dancing. So come with me, pilgrim; we
have a banquet to attend."

As if by magick, the shaking of her sistrum brings the very
walls to life. The wall relief's dancers and musicians with flutes,
harps, lutes, drums, cymbals, wooden clappers, and tambourines
now stream out, passing you, laughing in gay abandon, throwing
perfume-drenched flower petals for the goddess to walk upon.

The second Hypostyle Hall is now filled with the happy company. Against a sidewall is a long table laden with sumptuous
dishes of foods. The smell of freshly baked bread from emmer
wheat reaches your nostrils. A gathering of guests have arrived

and are now making their way towards the banquet table. They are dressed in semitransparent garments; on their wigged heads they wear unguent-perfumed wax cones. Between them weave muu-dancers wearing short white kilts and, on their heads, strange reed crowns. They perform amazing feats, leaping, twirling, and bending their bodies in time with the music.

Helping himself to figs stuffed with gazelle, you see your friend and guardian, Djehuty. His keen eyes survey the foodstuffs: roasted wild fowl sprinkled with tiny toasted seeds, crescent-shaped almond biscuits, cakes baked with dates and sweetened with golden honey, opened pomegranates revealing the luscious fruit within, great jars of barley beer and ewers of wine. Full luscious grapes are arranged in pyramidal shapes amidst piles of palm nuts and almonds. Choice cuts of roasted oxen are artfully arranged upon another table.

Lotus flowers and flower collars are being handed out by young girls, scantily dressed in just little beaded belts. Their golden bodies glisten with perfumed oil, attracting admiring glances from both male and female guests. Your head is swimming with excitement at the whole spectacle. Djehuty and Hathor laugh, but not unkindly, at your wonder.

The goddess takes your hand and leads you to the centre of the festivities and now dances with her arms raised and curved towards her head. In her left hand she still holds the bronze mirror, and now gazes into it, smiling, and sways in time to the rhythmic thump of a solo drumbeat. You find yourself copying her very movements; waves of energy flow up from the ground and surge through your body that serve to evoke ancient powers and memories. The drumbeat takes you deeper and deeper into other levels of consciousness. No other sound exists except for the drumbeat.

The guests look on, smiling and clapping their hands with joy, as you continue to spin and twirl and are at one with the dancers, full of the joy of life—a sort of radiant cakewalk of old Egyptian days. How supple are these dancers! They seem to have no bones. The guests are content just to witness the spectacle; it would not do to abandon all decorum and become part of the dance. Not in public anyway; such pleasures are best kept for the bedroom.

You hear two lovers say:

"How sweet is the name of Hathor! Without her to bring us together, life would be unbearable, like the wastes of the Red Land which receive no rain."

A merry musician chimes:

"Look kindly upon me, Mother, as I play thee this song, and drain many jugs of beer to thy honour, all night long."

The notes from the musicians contain multiple overtones that are steeped in powerful shamanic spiritual traditions. These notes impact upon your senses; the air around you forms a prism causing white light to refract the different colours of the rainbow. You now begin to sing. Your voice breaks up the harmonics of the musicians into specific sound frequencies that cascade the colours around you like a wonderful waterfall. You have found your signature note and the Universe reflects it back to you.

You are now dancing alone, but to a different rhythm. Gone are the guests, dancers, and musicians. Gone too is the joyous, beautiful goddess Hathor. Djehuty is now by your side as you still gently sway. He places his hands softly on your shoulders as if to say, "It is time to awaken from the dream." Before you now stands a woman with a strained expression that suggests to you more than gravity—almost anguish—of the soul and the spirit. Was this an echo of the ideal of joy in the time of the Ptolemies or in an age long before Khemit had felt their presence on its soils? That rapturous age of laughter, song and dance, and carefree spirit has faded.

The Temple of Hathor still holds the pale colours that here and there sing, but the rest is broken, almost haggard. The first hall is greyish white with a now-blackened roof from the soot of ancient

Christian fires as they sent their protestations to their one god in heaven.

Hathor's face looks down upon you, weary and sad—the Hathor of Denderah, the sad-eyed dweller on the columns of the first and second halls. Ruby red tears flow from her eyes. The tears that she has shed over millennia have dried up, only to give way to the sacrifice of her life-blood. At your feet you look down at a discarded mirror once consecrated to her, and hear Djehuty say:

"She will not see what she has become. Had she a veil, she would surely cover the face that witnessed the cruel evidence of early Christian ferocity."

From the gloomy courts you hear sobbing and whispering:

"Once I was worshipped, but I am worshipped no longer."

Civilisations ebb and flow and great empires rise up from the dust and crumble back into nothingness once their time has passed, and their glories forgotten. You know change is inevitable but that does not lessen the pain of loss—of those you have loved, of precious memories and knowledge. Where does it all go? Your heart weighs heavy with the tears you have not yet shed for your beloved Neters.

"O wondrous Hathor, I feel your loss and lament the passing of that once-great age when your grace and power flowed through the life-blood of this land. You have not been forgotten, as long as I and other worshippers have breath, you shall live within our hearts and be worshipped with the passion you deserve."

Djehuty is now standing behind you. He can add nothing to your thoughts; he just reminds you that is time for you to go. In silence you sadly construct your pylons and walk through the portal to your world of familiar regions. Utter your secret name to the gods and seal the door behind you.

TWELVE

LEGEND OF NUT

*The height of heaven and the stars [thereof] are obedient unto thee,
and thou makest to be opened the great gates [of the sky].*

E. A. WALLIS BUDGE, *LEGENDS OF THE EGYPTIAN GODS*

Shrines of the goddess Nut were not very numerous, but there was a Per-Nut, in Memphis, and a Het-Nut, in the Delta, and three rooftop chambers in the temple of Denderah called respectively Ant-en-Nut, Per-mest-en-Nut, and Per-netch-Nut-ma-Shu. It is to Denderah where the Path to Nut will take you to learn the truth of her being. It is said that she was the very first goddess to be worshipped and revered in the ancient land of Khemit.

The stellar goddess is usually depicted in the form of a woman holding a vase of water that indicates both her name and her nature; she sometimes wears on her head the horns and disk of the goddess Hathor, and holds in her hands a papyrus sceptre and the ankh, symbol of life.

However, we recognise the goddess better with the whole of her body and limbs bespangled with stars. The curious images of her in the Denderah chambers show a woman bent round in the form of a semicircle. Within the woman is Nut, and within this second body is a man that is bent round in such a way as to form an almost-complete circle.

One could say that the outer body of a woman is the heaven over which Ra travels, and that the inner body is the heaven through which the moon makes his way at night, while the male body within them is the almost-circular valley of the Duat. Another explanation could be that it is two women, the personification of the day and night skies.

However she is portrayed, Nut has absorbed the attributes of all the great mothers of the gods in the world.

In the scrolls found at Nag Hammadi in 1945, there is an entire chapter given by a goddess. This goddess uses the words "I AM" when talking to the people. She identifies herself as "I Am, and the Goddess of Thunder." The following is an excerpt from *The Thunder, Perfect Mind* and very reminiscent of the goddess Nut—the unmated mother:

"For I am the first and the last.
I am the honoured one and the scorned one.
I am the whore and the holy one.
I am the wife and the virgin.
I am the mother and the daughter.
I am the members of my mother.
I am the barren one and many are her sons.
I am she whose wedding is great, and have not taken a
    husband.
I am the midwife and she who does not bear.
I am the solace of my labour pains.
I am the bride and the bridegroom, and it is my husband who
    begot me.
I am the mother of my father and the sister of my husband
and he is my offspring.
I am the slave of him who prepared me.
I am the ruler of my offspring.
But he is the one who begot me before the time on a birthday
And he is my offspring in due time, and my power is from
    him.

I am the staff of his power in his youth, and he is the rod of
    my old age.
And whatever he wills happens to me.
I am the silence that is incomprehensible and the idea whose
    remembrance is frequent.
I am the voice whose sound is manifold and the word whose
    appearance is multiple.
I am the utterance of my name."

Mystically, the stars held great importance to the ancient
Egyptians, as they regarded all stars as gods. The heliacal setting
of a star in the west—Amenti—was looked upon as its "death,"
and the star would make its voyage through the portal to the Duat
or the Underworld where the god Ra journeyed each night, personified as the aged god Atum.

The ancient Egyptians have always been regarded as "flat
earth" people; the sky was above and below the earth, and they
perceived that their world was contained within a recognised
border. They believed the sky was held aloft at the four cardinal
points by pillars or mountain peaks that rose above the range creating the world's edge, and Nut the sky goddess supported the
heavenly bodies across which the sun god travelled every day.

During the early phase of Egypt's development, the seven stars
of Nut gave their names to the first nomes; this was during the period when time was measured by the stars. But Nut and her child
Set were considered unreliable because of their false timekeep-
ing, and as a result, were cast out by the Solarites in the name of
Osiris, who gradually took over from the lunar god Djehuty. This
glorified the god as the father of the child.

The constant clash between the cult of Set and the cult of
Horus split the land of Egypt in two, as first one, and then the
other, fought for supremacy.

However, the solar regime seemed to accomplish final victory,
and the Egyptians merged into the cult of Christendom. There are

still undertones in today's Christianity of the more ancient cult of goddess worship.

PATH TO NUT
Journey to Denderah Temple

Don your white robe and tie blue and white cords around your waist. This will be in respect of the Neter you will be working with.

Build your pylons and make the sign of the ankh in the air above your head. On the lintel of the portal, hieroglyphs of Nut will appear:

Commit them to memory. This symbol is charged; look at each mark and take it within. As you utter your secret name, your journey takes you to the second Hypostyle Hall that leads to the sacred shrine of Denderah Temple. This is a gateway that will take you to the heart of Nut's realm. You will learn how to focus on her energy as you are drawn in.

Waiting outside this hallowed place is Djehuty, who explains that the stellar goddess Nut will be putting on an amazing display of her coming into being and you must make your way to the roof above.

Leaving the sacred shrine area, you retrace your steps back through to the second Hypostyle Hall, and begin your climb up an extraordinary narrow and worn stairway. You glide effortlessly up these stairs; subliminally your energy is taken from you almost like a sacrifice as you make your way towards the divine.

Pausing, you look at the beautifully sculptured low relief scenes that appear on the walls the entire length of this staircase. They depict the most important ritual-procession of the temple—that of the New Year of Nut—moving onwards with Pharaoh himself at its head. From the very stone emerge priests proffering long incense burners, initiates of the Mysteries followed by standard-bearers, all making their way up the stairs. The intoxicating aroma of incense and the steady beat of a drum excite your inner being.

Walking in procession these final steps to the rooftop with the priests of Denderah, you step out of the gloom with them into the brilliance of Ra and a sky of cobalt blue. You pause and look down at the lush, emerald green fields below that contrast dramatically with the desert sands beyond. You stand for a moment drinking in the colour.

A hum of praying and praising voices are hushed. All else is silent as the Sem Priest utters an invocation to the heavens:

"In the unremembered ages,
In the nights that are forgotten,
Downward through the starry cosmos,
From a far-off constellation,
Fell the beautiful night-enchantress.
She, born of the mystery of heavenly stardust,
Out of Nun's watery celestial abyss.
We summon thee."

There is shifting in the heavens as though a storm is breaking, then the firmament above you turns an inky blue, followed by darkness and an eerie silence. In front of the temple, four huge pillars of cloud stretch from earth to heaven—these pillars are actually supporting the sky! One is of molten gold, another of pure silver, the third of lapis lazuli, and the fourth of carnelian. Between them runs a road of radiant light ending in magnificent splendour, and in the midst of this light spins Ra in all his glory. Then, he is gone! The light of Luna Djehuty rains down.

There follows another great silence. The heavens now move and shift whilst the white-robed priests bow their heads and weep. Even Pharaoh lowers his head.

From the far reaches of the heavens a sound is heard. The priests stop weeping and begin to sing a song of exaltation together with a voice that intones sounds of celestial spheres, of harmonious spinning patterns, ever changing the designs of heaven, and from it is born the star body, paradise mother. A strong scent of frankincense, myrrh, cypress, and jasmine fills the air.

In the moonlight and the starlight, Nut's form sparkles like a diamond. Her crystal eyes shine like orbs. Her giant body arches over the sky. Beloved Nut of the starry skies speaks:

"I am blessed by Nun, father of all gods who gave me Sothis as my kingdom." Shining splendid is her prize. All begin to chant:

"Nut, enchantress of the stellar heavens,
Nut, goddess of the seven stars."

Her huge starry form descends and hovers above your heads. When she speaks, her voice is now likened to the delicate plucking of harp strings, each note falling like a tiny star around you.

"When the brotherhood of man was formed, my star-cult grew in numbers, thus establishing the first earth nomes that were based on Siriun cosmic lore. All was well in the land, my children. You were happy to honour me at the close of Ra's day in the west land. You were happy when I gathered the great sun into my sacred body, spilling out the starry night."

A sudden change in her voice makes the heavens grow dark and shift moodily above. She continues:

"But then the heavens were thus divided, and you split my land of Khemit in two, giving my beloved firstborn Set the southland, manifesting my light, whilst I ruled the north. But let it not be forgotten that *I* was the first timekeeper. Do I not hold aloft the pillars of the sky supporting all the heavenly bodies?"

Everyone, including Pharaoh, shifts nervously as the goddess chastises them.

"It is true that you continue to love me nightly in my dark skies, but then you replaced me with Djehuty, the lunar god!"

You look at your guardian in surprise, wondering what is going to happen next.

Djehuty strides forward and, raising himself up to meet the eyes of Nut, replies:

"Yes, it is true, my lady, that *I*, Djehuty, replaced you, and in doing so I gave Khemit twenty-eight lunar houses, thirty-six Nomes, and thus created the lunar calendar that mirrored the land of Khemit. It is also true that I transferred to earth the celestial symbolism of the heavens as the Circle of Nut. But, dear Lady Nut, fugitive were my lunar timings, unstable were my lunar days, so *I* too was cast out. It was then the dark god faced the light, and so was phased in the solar day."

As Djehuty speaks, the body of Nut explodes back into millions of stars held aloft by her four magnificent pillars, and between them again runs a road of light culminating in a glorious fusion of colours, and in the midst of these colours the round orb of Ra is reborn, heralding another day. The manifestation of deity is breathtaking.

Djehuty ushers you to one of the roof temples that is devoted to Nut in all her guises. Her poses are reminiscent of yoga, her contorted body swallowing the sun at night, surrounded by her stars, and giving birth to the sun again in the morning. In the dim light, the colours vibrate and you feel her pulse within. You look up at her glorious face and see her weeping, but they are not tears; they are stars that fall around you in great pools. Nut speaks solely to you:

"I am the first mother who gave birth to the child of chaos, Set. I held him close to me and fed him the milk of stardust. He reigned supreme with me, I the unmated mother! All was well, even when I had to share my realm with Djehuty. But when the usurper Osiris was introduced into my land of Khemit, my son and I were cast aside. Osiris took Isis as his consort and his gift to her was my realm that included my star, Sothis. She took everything from me, even my title of the Goddess of Infinite Space and Time. Know this, O pilgrim—when you gaze upon the image of Isis and Horus, you really are gazing at me, Nut, and my child Set."

You move close to the wall and rest your face against hers and there locked within the stone is truth. You could stay here listening to the history of the ages unfold, but Djehuty tells you it is time to leave this other world of temples of the Mysteries, goddess and her stars, and together you wind your way down a spiralling staircase towards the main temple complex below.

As you make your way down the stairs of Denderah Temple, they have an unwinding effect on your psyche, very much in contrast with those on the east side of the temple that drew you up.

Pharaoh and his retinue of priests are also descending, but there are no prayers said; all you hear is the steady striking of a drum in time to your heartbeat.

Before walking through the Hypostyle Hall, you catch the drift of incense as it wafts through the temple, and pausing, you look into the inner shrine where you hope to catch a glimpse of Hathor, but Djehuty reminds you that it is time for you to go. Construct your pylons and walk through the portal to your world of familiar regions. Utter your secret name to the gods and seal the door behind you.

THIRTEEN

LEGEND OF SETEREION

Thou art the Great One in Abydos, thou art the Morning Star which appears in the eastern part of heaven, to which thy twin Horus of the Tuat has given his body. O great and exalted one among the imperishable stars, thou shalt never perish.

UTTERANCE 509, BOOK OF THE DEAD

There is a place in Egypt that we have *all* visited, even if we have never been there in this or any other life. On one level it can be found at Abydos, within the ruins of a mysterious building commonly known as the Osireion; at another level it exists somewhere in the dark and torn places of the heart, and is approached through the cold passages leading from the back of the mind. We may never have set foot in Egypt, or even so much as studied its imagery from the safety of our couches, but we have all made journeys into the tangible night of that odd and eerie temple. We are all, in our own way, initiates of its mysteries.

The Osireion lies behind the Great Temple of Seti I. No one has ever been entirely sure about its purpose, and there are those who believe, with justification, that it may be as old as or older than even the Great Pyramid or the Great Sphinx of Giza. Architecturally it is unique; its design and its gigantic blocks differ from any structure previously discovered in Egypt. It lies sunk into a depression on a level with the water table, and is comprised of a central hall surrounded by water-filled ditches, containing a central "island" that once held a single sarcophagus. Opinions are divided as to whether it was a mortuary temple or a cenotaph; with no hard evidence, it is linked with the god Osiris, hence its official name. But no one who has ever been there under the ink-black sky scattered with diamonds remains in doubt as to its sanctity. In the Thirteenth Dynasty, when the Osireion was already ancient, Pharaoh Neferhotep erected a boundary stele comparable to the warning signs you get around nuclear sites today, commanding that no one should even set foot in the area. Whether it was too sacred or too dangerous, he neglected to explain. Sometimes the two are inseparable.

In this place, if you descend the steps, you encounter holiness so black that you have to feel your way through it, in a silence so profound that it makes your eardrums thud. And as you enter the chamber, another heavily laden kind of darkness overtakes you, a dangerous mass, a Presence with an intent beyond your mortal comprehension. It touches on your shoulders and tells you that you are not alone, while all around, you can glimpse slowly moving, indecipherable shapes which approach and study your every breath. Few can stay down there for long. Few would be mad enough, or wise enough, to visit in the first place. That is the Osireion, as many (perhaps mistakenly) call it. But we will know it as the Setereion.

As we enter and study its secrets, we will find that these are also *our* secrets, sealed within our psyches in a place of darkness that is buried beneath the desert of what passes for living in these modern times. What we will learn in this place is the magick of that darkness, the meaning of those shapes and Presence, and the light, change, healing, and strength that can arise from such knowledge. On magickal levels, we will put Osiris to rest at last, and restore his archrival Set to his proper place in all the worlds. On human levels, we will learn to awaken those forgotten or neglected parts of ourselves and become strong, magickal beings.

PATH TO SETEREION

Journey to Abydos

Don your white robe and tie black and red cords around your waist. This will be in respect of the Neter you will be working with.

Build your pylons and make the sign of the ankh in the air above your head. On the lintel of the portal, hieroglyphs of Set will appear:

Commit them to memory. This symbol is charged; look at each mark and take it within. As you utter your secret name, your journey takes you to the Setereion, hallowed place of Set. This is a gateway that will take you to the heart of his realm. You will learn how to focus on his energy as you are drawn in.

Djehuty is watching out for you in the gloomy darkness just above the entrance to the Setereion. You are so pleased when he takes your hand and guides you down a steep slope far below the main-earth level. Then he leaves you, saying:

"Few can stay down there for long."

You now walk alone along a subterranean passage. Within the walls is a menacing sound and an funguslike odour hangs heavy and deathlike in the air.

A strange radiance guides you along, emitting just enough light for you to make out ancient wall reliefs depicting strange boat people who came to the land of Khemit long, long ago. The corridor then twists abruptly to the left and slopes down to a central aisle. With intent beyond your mortal comprehension, something touches your shoulder, making you realise that you are not alone. You flinch in surprise and then glimpse an indecipherable shape slowly approaching, studying your every move. Djehuty's words echo in your head:

"Few can stay down there for long."

Then out of the gloom you are confronted by the wolf god, Wep-wa-wet in all his splendour. He greets you, beckoning you to follow. By now your heart is racing, and you begin to sweat with cold fear. Together you walk along this passageway that appears to come to a dead end, but concealed within the sandstone is a doorway that opens at the god's touch.

As you pass through the doorway, you find yourself on the edge of a causeway, and leading off it are fourteen rooms that surround an island. Velvet blackness cloaks you, and you pause briefly, taking stock of your bearings and allowing your eyes to adjust to the gloom. Suddenly wall sconces combust into light, giving you a glimpse of dark red granite walls hung with red and gold banners that gently balloon by an inner wind within them. It feels like a space which is not of this world, but emanating from a dimension untouched by human thought and action. You wonder what lies ahead.

The air is heavy with sweet aromas like water-drenching sun-hot sandstone, freshly cut hay in grasslands, sandstorms of the annual Khamsin, and sodden wood after rain.

In this odd and eerie temple, you can hear the many voices of past initiates who have received their secret lessons and instruction into the darker mysteries from the Priesthood of Set, who remain ever faithful, but unseen, in the Neter's presence. You hear them make solemn pledges to their god and, as they make their pledges, they lay their naked hearts before him and make promises to the future.

You continue to stand in the shadows and, as the voices fade, a silence cloaks you.

The floor of the centre island is of black quartz crystal that reflects a dimly lit image. Your attention shifts and, gazing upwards, a dark form materializes. The great god Set is before you, ever wakeful, ever watchful in his sanctum. You bravely cross the causeway to the island to meet this Neter.

He sits upon a regal high throne made of the gold from Nubty. On his head he wears the double crown of Upper and Lower Egypt. His face is chiselled with fine emotion. You have seen this face before.

From his broad chest hangs a collar of electrum. He wears a tunic of black, red, and gold that is gently defused by the black flames licking and spluttering the edge of his podium.

In his left hand he holds the uwas sceptre, sculptured in his dog-form likeness. His bright green eyes shine forth upon you, and in the glimmering flicker of firelight he bestows his gift of inner sight upon you.

Silence continues to reign. Then, Set breaks this silence with a voice likened to winds roaring, each distinct with its own message. The notes resound across the quartz floor as the words engulf you, filling your spirit as he bestows the gift of sound upon you.

He then steps lightly down from his platform and, walking across the quartz floor through the flickering black flames, he stands tall and beautiful before you.

You feel his breath on your face that is likened to sweet almond oil as he bestows the blessing of smell upon you.

Reaching out, he touches your heart, gripping your emotions. By his action his hand dissolves right through you as he bestows the blessing of touch upon you.

The very nearness to him, and the solitary five thousand years he has endured in this world alone, makes you shed tears of sorrow, tears that could fill an ocean.

From the shadows you can hear the weeping and lamenting of cries for his lost children, whose souls now assemble around you.

You are unable to speak to Set directly, but he fuses his thoughts with yours and reveals aeons of his knowledge of the ancient past and present, and of the times to come.

"O Seeker of the Mysteries," he whispers, "Bravely have you sought to find me. You have passed your test on many of the paths, but this is not your final one. You must venture further northward, seeking always a star to guide you. Djehuty and I will be with you. See the reeling stars above you; may Mesxet descend upon you, as the stellar meets the terra, on the morrow and the next night, when my mother greets her soul child, like a red and burning nova. From the heartland of my kingdom, may you reach your higher mental plane."

Then he is gone. You stand there in the blackness. All around is total stillness. You are alone on this island. Nowhere is the sacred priesthood and gone is Set from your presence. Has this encounter been just a dream? You then hear whispers again from the shadows:

"This is no ordinary mortuary temple to a god of pure stasis you have visited, O Seeker of the Mysteries, but a place of pure chaos, and this is Set's sanctuary of confusion."

You have seen the inner sanctum of the Setereion and revealed your soul to the Great One. He has looked upon you, a fragile earthly being, and taken you to the heights of stellar realms, and promised to be with you always.

From the crypt you go forth in silence and look for your guardian Djehuty through the darkness. From behind you, he touches your left shoulder and says:

"You're not alone. Let us leave this place of mystery and return to the bank above where you can talk to me, your guardian."

As you numbly walk along the darkened corridor, you are relieved at long last to be able to talk to Djehuty about your ordeal. You tell him how you laid bare your soul's secrets and describe how Set reached inside your mortal body, and with a touch so light and invisible you felt him shake the heavens until his mother's stars trembled about you.

Djehuty smiles warmly at you, and for seven nights and days you stay there, in the desert by the Setereion. Together you look on the splendour of the sunrises and the many varied sunsets that move through the purple twilight.

You gaze up at the body of Nut through the stardust, feasting on the stellar magick as the Great Bear swings above you. You hear the desert beyond calling to you. Again your soul has been lost in the magick of this ancient land of Khemit, and as you look searchingly at Djehuty for more answers, he shakes his head indicating "another time."

It is time to go. Construct your pylons and walk through the portal to your world of familiar regions. Utter your secret name to the gods and seal the door behind you.

FOURTEEN

LEGEND OF OSIRIS

May you grant power in the sky, might on earth and vindication in the realm of the dead...to go in and out without hindrance at all the gates of the Netherworld.

BOOK OF THE DEAD: HYMN TO OSIRIS

He is known by many names—Wasir, W'sr, Asar, to name but a few. He is described as a god in anthropomorphic form holding two sceptres in the shape of a "crook" and a "flail," wearing a conical crown decorated with two feathers called the atef crown.

But, we are not really describing Osiris at all! This is a description of an earlier god originally worshipped in the mid-Delta in the Lower Egyptian Nome 9. His name was Andjety, which means "He who comes from the Andjety waters," called Busiris.

One is prone to imagine, without being able to prove it, that this Andjety had once been a chieftain who fell in battle while fighting against the eastern Bedouins and became deified after his death. However that may be, he later gave his form to Osiris, as the double name Osiris-Andjety indicates. Osiris then completely replaced him and received from him the description "Lord of Busiris."

As early as the beginning of the Fourth Dynasty, Pharaoh Snofre, the builder of the first true pyramid tomb, is pictured wearing the atef crown of Andjety. The close relationship between the god Andjety and the monarch is also apparent from the earliest references in the Pyramid Texts, where the king's power as a universal ruler is much enhanced by his being associated with Andjety, keeping order over the eastern districts.

Perhaps Andjety is an embodiment of sovereignty through his symbols of office. As such, he would readily be absorbed into the nature of Osiris.

But it doesn't end here. Andjety is very much evident in a funerary text as well. The idea that he is responsible for rebirth in the afterlife is almost certainly the reason for the substitution of the two feathers instead of the bovine uterus, symbol for rebirth in early writings of his name in the Pyramid Texts.

There is an obvious identification in the underworld between Andjety and Osiris as ruler. For this reason, in the Temple of Sety I at Abydos, the king is depicted burning incense to the god Andjety-Osiris, who holds the crook sceptre, wears two feathers in his headband, and is accompanied by Isis.

"Lord of the Abju (the watery abyss and also semen) and Lord of the Earth. He also holds dominion over the soil that reflects the role of water in fructifying the earth thus making possible the development of vegetation, communications, and civilizing mankind. He was also considered the supreme god of wisdom and magick, and the keeper of the divine laws."

The above is not a description of Osiris—it is of Enki! For those who are interested in the Egyptian-Sumerian parallels, we must look at the comparisons between Osiris and the Nile River, and Enki who bestows the powers of the fertile sweet waters upon Sumer. The only difference between these two gods is that Osiris dies and is resurrected annually when the Nile floods, whereas Enki's watery power never dies, and is a living joyous force.

In art, Enki is represented as a seated god with a beard, wearing a long wig and cap surmounted with many ribbons, and garbed in a long robe. In early representations of Osiris, he is depicted the same, except that in his hands he holds the crook and flail.

In 1869, the French-German scholar Jules Oppert led a team of archaeologists in Iraq to discover traces of Sumerian artefacts, speculating that it was Sumer and not Egypt that was the legendary "one true beginning" of world civilisation. Bearing this in mind, there is every reason to believe that the Sumerians played a dominant role in the early stages of civilisation in Ur- Egypt, bringing their own gods with them.

Not content with usurping the identity of Andjety, Osiris then moved on to the predynastic town of Abdjw—Abydos, the sacred site of Khentamenthes, who was the original god of the dead. Primarily he was represented as a sitting dog (akin to the Set animal), the protector of the necropolis. The irony is that his name "Khentamenthes" signifies "First of the Westerners" (that is, of the dead).

But Abydos did not become an historical memory to an ancient dog god, but gained rather a timeless, ever-present importance, based on an imported god called Osiris.

So who then was Osiris? Perhaps the path to this multifaceted Neter will give us a clue. Or perhaps not!

PATH TO OSIRIS
The Passion Play

Don your white robe and tie black and green cords around your waist. This will be in respect of the Neter you will be working with.

Build your pylons and make the sign of the ankh in the air above your head. On the lintel of the portal, hieroglyphs of Osiris appear:

Commit them to memory. This symbol is charged; look at each mark and take it within. As you utter your secret name, your journey takes you to the desert just beyond Abydos.

The sands stretch into infinity, broken only by the many mirages, which emerge out of the shimmering air, only to disappear with the blink of an eye. The silence is heavy and tinged with a sadness you cannot hope to comprehend—yet. Suddenly the howling of a dog breaks into this reverie and a voice behind you speaks; it is Djehuty:

"He was known as Khentamenthes. He came from the dog group of Candides, and was the protector of this resting place. An ancient king built a temple to him, a shrine of mud, reeds, and wicker. This was his region; he held supreme dominion over all the winds of heaven, till the sun and moon changed places, and the Night-sun set eastward, till the sky was red with sunrise, till the pallid moon and the Night-sun rose above the sombre Abju."

As you look around, the desert sand blows away, revealing mound upon mound of small terra cotta clay pots. Djehuty tells you that they are the libation vessels left by the many mourners who came to this sacred place to honour their loved ones, who were all in the protection of the dog god.

You walk the land together with Djehuty amongst the spiritual resting place of thousands. All around you the earth is reddened with the many earth-fired vessels, making the earth appear as if it is stained with the blood of many, sacrifices that were offered up for the fertility of the land. Stooping down, you gather up two tiny cups of ancient giving, and with your two hands uplifted, you look skyward.

Deep within you, you feel both joy and sadness; a tingling sensation passes from the vessels to your fingers. With a sense of knowing in your being, you send a joyous prayer to heaven, then you drop the tiny clay pots earthward into the soft white sand of Abju.

You look expectantly towards the horizon; something awaits but you know not what. A voice bids you farther into the desert and your feet carry you deeper into its heart. A strange sensation sweeps through your body as you hold your breath in anticipation. Your vision appears blurred at first, then it clears to reveal the apparition before you.

Gliding forward like a phantom appears the wondrous god Osiris, clothed in fine white linen. On his head he wears the crown of Upper Khemit; in his hands he holds the crook, flail, and sceptre. A wondrous aroma of honey, jasmine, and lotus is all around you.

A cry wells up in your throat as you gaze upon this divine god before you. Osiris speaks; his voice is womanlike:

"Regard At' Ur the river!" he gestures. "Behold the waters; see how they are swollen by inundation. Behold again as the waters fall. Now behold the birds and insects." From nowhere, butterflies and birds swoop between you and Osiris, who has now wandered through the paradise that has been created in the sands around you.

A load roar splits the air as the god Set arrives on the scene.

"What have you done? Do you place yourself above me? Am I not a god in equal status with you? Are you saying that this is all your creation? Dear brother, you weave a seductive tale that promises much but crumbles under closer scrutiny. Why won't you share this prize with me? What are you fearful of losing?"

Osiris answers with haughty coolness. His complete indifference is evident, his mood changed.

"True, our father gave it to us both, but we have a right to choose how we divide it, a pledge for good or for evil."

You hang on every word as Osiris's voice echoes across the desertscape. He watches the fury of Set, his sibling, and unwisely draws closer to speak to him. But only the gods know what is coming next.

Osiris, feigning a yawn, waves his right hand in gesture, dismissing his troubled brother to leave his garden saying:

"This is the world I am revealing to you, my dear brother; a land in peace awaits you where all the gates stand open and welcome you. But if you come in warlike vengeance, rage, and hatred, then I order you to go now as I am weary of your quarrels and your thirst for bloodshed, and I tire of your threats for vengeance."

This only serves to infuriate Set more, and like the "bull of his mother," he bellows:

"All is not well between us, brother. I have listened to your empty verbiage and your words of stasis, and long have I waited for this moment."

Hunching his massive shoulders and lifting his golden sword, Set rushes headlong towards Osiris, who still has his right hand extended regally, holding his sceptre. Set's mighty sword cuts right through it, making the hand disappear from his thin wrist and sending the sceptre flying across the garden. So complete is this act that Osiris just stands in amazement, still clasping the crook and flail in his left hand.

You sit amazed, unable to take in the sight before you, and look sideways at Djehuty, who is completely absorbed in the spectacle and does not bat an eyelid.

Osiris reels back, screaming and clutching his handless stump in anguish. But before Osiris reaches the edge of the garden, Set is right there behind him and, seizing his stump as a handle, he drags his brother to the centre of the lawn throwing him full-length sprawling, where he lies on the grass shrieking: "O dear brother, please spare me!"

As Set stands there in all his splendour, dressed in colours of red, black, and yellow, he laughingly tosses his red tresses, saying as sweet and childlike as ever:

"Now you fear me, gentle brother, as you lie down, pleading and writhing like a cut snake." Set then screams out, shaking with savage laughter.

You want to cry out: "Spare Osiris!" but you stay seated, not daring to move.

With his one remaining hand, Osiris reaches out to paw at Set, who then grabs his brother's left arm, inspecting it like a butcher inspects a piece of meat.

Echoes of a past audience scream across the sands of time:

"Cut it off! Kill him, kill him!" Around you mass an audience of spectators, including the great Pharaoh Rameses II, whose mood has also swung against this god. All sit upright to look and listen. Set has stirred their souls to passion and, with the blood lust of the many, he now moulds them all to hatred.

Deftly he raises his gold sword once more and, with a casual sweeping forward, passes it through Osiris's limb, causing that hand to disappear as well. Triumphantly Set holds his magickal blade above his head as his brother falls at his feet.

Feebly Osiris tries to rise up but has no support left in him and writhes, kicking out his legs in futile spasm. His head whips forlornly sideways, screaming for mercy. The audience sits enthralled at the spectacle happening before them.

Set's laughter fills the atmosphere whilst his brother continues to cry: "Help me, help me!"

All watch on, knowing a deeper tale is unfolding. Meanwhile Set points his sword again at the body, cutting it into three pieces then, picking up each body part and hurling it out to the captivated audience. But all they receive is gold dust and not their god's body at all. Roaring with frenzy, they grab at the precious ore floating like a fine mist through the air. The crowd then surges forward, clamouring and shouting:

"Give us a charm, a talisman!"

Set hears voices calling to him for the greatest prize of magick.

"What more do you want? Haven't I already given you enough of your dear and wondrous saviour? What other prize do you crave?" he teases.

"A talisman, give us a talisman!" they call in unison.

"So you want *all* his magick then?"

The audience continues screaming for the utmost charm of any great god who controls the darkest forces of the Apep daemon. They want the fourteenth segment, the only fragment worth possessing, the only piece never recovered and never found by his sister Nephthys, as the god Set had thrown the phallus member into the watery Nile to be eaten by a fish! Set denies them their prize, but still they roar for this treasure:

"Give us the Talisman of Osiris!"

Set reaches down through the sodden linen of the now-blood-soaked, limbless body of Osiris and laughs in wild abandon as the crowd begs:

"Give it to us! Give us the power of his phallus!"

Still Set ignores their pleas with pleasure, and cries to the pharaoh:

"As your God of Darkness, I offer his phallus of magick to the greatest Pharaoh on this earth! A gift from one mighty god to another!"

Set now bounds toward his patron and places the mark of Osiris at the feet of Rameses, who gathers up this powerful relic. Spellbound beneath paint and powder, Rameses smiles down at this prize; believing it to be a magickal symbol, he holds it up for all to gaze on.

Set is now well pleased that his gift has been accepted and returns to the scene to complete more acts of vengeance on his brother, who is still alive but now in limbo. From his eyes the tears are flowing, his body shrunk and dwindled, drowning in a pool of life-blood that is fast becoming gold dust.

With a swing of his sword, Set severs Osiris's head. He stands there victorious, holding up his final trophy. Osiris's tongue now hangs speechless, but his eyes still swivel wildly, looking upon the world he once ruled. As they dull and cloud over, Set throws the head of Osiris directly towards you. The shock and surprise of this action makes you reel back in horror. Tears flow copiously from his eyes, only to turn into gold dust floating away on the breath of the wind. A once-mighty god reduced to this! You cannot comprehend such a thing happening; the Neters are eternal and unchanging.

Set whispers in your ear:

"Eternal? Unchanging? Why do you compel us to dwell in a mythic land of your imaginings, pilgrim? Your static perception of life serves no purpose. Perpetual sunshine only creates deserts. By shutting yourself away in your 'paradisiacal' little world, do you think you can keep the forces of change at bay? Wake up from your dream and face the truth—*face yourself*."

Set's laughter echoes through your head. You find yourself back in the empty desert wastes. They have all disappeared, even your guardian. It was all an illusion. You are convinced of this. Or are you? You feel shattered, unsure of the truth. What to do now?

"Whose truth have you been following, pilgrim, and are you capable of thinking for yourself?"

Set's words gently taunt you as he places his hands on your shoulders. He turns you around and there before you is the entire theatrical company of this sacred drama. Shining Osiris stands tall and complete. How can this be? This wondrous god fell prey to his murderous brother's rage time and time again. It was a history that was played out across aeons and was enshrined within the sacred scripts of this ancient land. You feel confused. The divine assembly stands silent and majestic as they await your verdict. Djehuty offers a small bow in your direction and invites your deliberations.

It is time to leave, and as you visualise your great pylon in front of you to walk through its portal to your world of familiar regions, you think back on all that has disturbed you. Is it a truth you have not been aware of?

Now utter your secret name to the gods, and seal the door behind you.

FIFTEEN

LEGEND OF THE LABYRINTH

I am Sobek, who dwelleth amid his terrors. I am Sobek,
and I seize [my prey] like a ravening beast.
I am the great Fish which is in Kamui.
I am the Lord to whom bowings and prostrations
are made in Sekhem.

BOOK OF THE DEAD, THE CHAPTER OF MAKING THE TRANSFORMATION
INTO THE CROCODILE GOD (SOBEK)

In 1912, the renowned professor of ancient Egypt, Ahmed Fakhry, commented on the vast size of the labyrinth in Fayoum: "This immense building must have been about 300 meters [984 feet] long and 244 meters [800 feet] wide, large enough to hold the great temples of Karnak and Luxor."

It was thought that the labyrinth could have been an administrative centre, but Alan B. Lloyd rejected this idea in "The Egyptian Labyrinth" in *Journal of Egyptian Archaeology* (56:1970, pp. 81–100). He noted that stone was used to construct only two types of buildings in ancient Egypt: mortuary installations and temples. Palaces and administrative buildings were built of mud brick. Lloyd added that "the Labyrinth was certainly not intended by its builder as a tomb; for the monarchs of the Twelfth Dynasty as well as some of the rulers of the Thirteenth Dynasty built pyramid tombs."

The ground plan and the individual parts of this building cannot be fully described because it is divided among the regions or administrative districts known as sepats or nomes, of which there are forty-two, each having a vast hall allotted to it by name. Besides these halls, it contained temples of all the Egyptian gods; and furthermore, Amenemhet III placed within the forty shrines several pyramids, each with a height of forty cubits and an area at the base of four acres. It is only when the visitor is already exhausted with walking that he reaches the bewildering maze of passages. Moreover, there are rooms in lofty upper stories reached by inclines, and porches from which flights of ninety stairs lead down to the ground. Inside are columns of sandstone, images of gods, statues of kings, and figures of monsters. Some of the halls are laid out in such a way that when the doors open, there is a terrifying rumble of thunder within. Incidentally, most of the building has to be traversed in darkness. Again, there are other massive structures outside the wall of the labyrinth.

It has twelve roofed courts, with doors facing one another, six to the north and six to the south, and in a continuous line. There are double sets of chambers in it, some underground and some above, and their number is three thousand; there are fifteen hundred of each.

It is said that the ancient kings built the labyrinth in the beginning for the holy crocodiles. The road to this labyrinth is made underground, and as he made his way through the maze, his old self was symbolically stripped off, much as a snake sheds its skin.

After the trials of the dark winding ways, he would reach the centre, the place of initiation and a rebirth into his "new life."

Like all initiates of old, he is conducted to the place of death, the underworld as the shady side of life—like Jung's shadow function, the place of unconsciousness that we visit every night in deep sleep, where may be found that which is needful for the next stage of our journey, and where we may leave behind that which is no longer required. He knows routes there, which allow return, the return out of the labyrinth, bringing back the revealed riches—the way to enlightenment is through taking a step into the dark.

Our awareness opens us to the sacredness of such moments, of unexpected silences, of those in-between times that are strangely frightening and those we so often try to hurry past. But in doing this, we never really know what may lie on the other side of any threshold.

This path will be a true test for you, the seeker, as you negotiate your way through the labyrinth. There will be moments when soul gazes directly at soul, where your thoughts and actions are mirrored. Such times are at once sublime and profoundly annihilating as the god within awakes from his slumber and drinks deeply from the chalice of your soul.

On this path you will gain an insight into the origins of this great maze and, as you traverse into disorienting chaos, you will ask yourself if you can stay the course. It is indeed an initiatory pathworking that harks back to ancient times, when these places were indeed used for ceremonies and rituals of initiation, rebirth, and rites of passage.

PATH TO SOBEK

Journey to the Labyrinth

Don your white robe and tie a purple cord around your waist. This will be in respect of the Neter you will be working with.

Build your pylons and make the sign of the ankh in the air above your head. On the lintel of the portal, hieroglyphs of Sobek appear.

Commit them to memory. This symbol is charged; look at each mark and take it within. As you utter your secret name, your journey takes you to the great labyrinth where you will commune with the god Sobek. You will learn how to focus on his energy as you are drawn in.

The rays of Ra beat mercilessly down, causing everything around you to shimmer in a heat haze. The figure of Djehuty emerges out of this haze to greet you. You are thankful to be ushered to the shade of a palm grove that surrounds a huge lake.

"This is the creation of Amen-em-het the first. He made clever use of the numerous underground springs in the area, uniting them into one large watery mass." Djehuty points it out to you.

You look upon the vast tranquil waters that resemble a tideless inland sea surrounded by clumps of red poppies and palms, heavy with luscious dates just ripe for picking. The green and red contrasts with the barren dry desert beyond.

Still gazing upon the waters, you notice something moving, getting closer, a dark shape just submerged below the surface. You move backwards instinctively towards Djehuty who laughingly explains that it is the sacred lake to Sobek and, as in Kom Ombos, the many reptiles after his likeness swim there.

As you continue to look across this perfect stretch of water, under a perfect cobalt blue sky, you find it hard to imagine this lake teaming with crocodiles, each sacred, each loved, and all under the protection of their patron god Sobek. You recall Djehuty telling you in Kom Ombos how each of these beloved crocodiles has a name and is lovingly reared by the wahab priests.

Looking beyond the lake, through the heat haze you see an enormous mastaba. Like a magnet you are drawn to it, quite forgetting that you are with your guardian Djehuty, and you make a mad dash for this massive monument built entirely of red mud brick. To your amazement, Djehuty has already reached the entrance and is busy speaking in low whispers to an old guardian priest:

"I am Keeper of the Inner Levels. I know the secrets of Light and Darkness of the Sacred Mystery School." The guardian looks at Djehuty with eyes of wonder, and bowing low, he replies:

"I am honoured, my lord, and bid you welcome. But what of this other person with you?"

"A seeker and pilgrim who is an old soul who has been returned to us." Djehuty explains.

"My lord, forbidden are these ancient dwellings to those other than the initiated. You know that within them are buried the pharaohs who built the labyrinth to Lord Sobek, the great god of mystery, and cousin to the dark god Set."

"The pilgrim is on a quest and seeks initiation into the higher mysteries of Khemit."

"Of course, my lord."

The guardian of the labyrinth readily understands and once again bows low to the Neter. Turning to you, he says:

"I pray thee, enter and walk among the ancient Neters, marvel at the pillared hallways and pause in the many splendid courtyards. But take care to read the signs, and do not believe all that is said to you."

As you walk away from order and into chaos, where no one will be there to guide you through this puzzle, this mighty labyrinth, you hear the priest repeat:

"Take care to read the signs, and do not believe all that is said to you."

Down and down you creep through the twilight along corridors, passing many crypts and caverns that beckon to you to "enter." Each turning you make leads to more confusing, winding tunnels. An inner voice within you is crying out for help, but no helper hears your plea. You are truly alone and can only rely upon yourself. Not a comfortable state of being, is it?

Deeper and deeper into the bowels of the labyrinth you wander. Then a loud voice booms at you like thunder that stirs not only you, but also every spirit within this darkened sanctum:

"Hasten back to your city, back to all who are faint-hearted."

You recall hearing a voice like that before, and with a similar message, but you retaliate, again saying:

"I will not listen to you, as you do not scare me. I will continue with my venture; I will find the inner sanctum and *I* shall be my guide in darkness. I have come here to face my demons and prove my worth amongst the priesthood!"

You twist and turn to face the direction of the voice that now laughs at you, calling you to follow, but all you can hear is the voice of the old guardian priest saying, "Take care to read the signs, and do not believe all that is said to you."

Not daunted, fearing nothing, you move through the blackness, being touched by the many spirits. You feel their soft hands and hear their whispers; they speak the language of the Old Ones that takes you back to the First Time. But a voice whispers to you:

"This is not the right time; you must wait, you must search on, and you must listen to our reasoning, listen to words of wisdom from the great ones in the darkness. For it is said of this dark place that all the nobles assembled here yearly, ranked together with priest and priestess, where gifts were offered to the Neters asking for guidance, justice, and order."

You hear their voices echo through the hallways, and listen as they relate an ancient history. You feel the moistened bodies of phantoms that resemble the spirit of the great Apophis slithering around you with all the stealth of evil. They hiss in unison:

"We give you a riddle, O Seeker of the Mysteries: Life is white, and death is darkened, life and death are drawn in circles, ever-diminishing concentric circles, a confusing mass of blind alleys that mirror images, back and forth." You can see the glow from their scaly bodies as they slither ever nearer to you.

"If you dare to follow us, we will tell you all you desire. We will show you wonderful things, earthling, as only we know the secret of immortal life. Come, come with us. We'll reward you by giving you the golden ankh of all wisdom."

You hear yourself saying: "How very beguiling you are, but I must not listen to your words as I feel that you are lying to me. I do not believe you have this ankh." As you utter these words, you watch the phantoms slither back into the blackness.

Then without warning, the ground sags like a sky-cloud under your weight. All becomes very strange as the earth bends and makes crackling noises beneath your feet. Then, like clouds being swept away from heaven, you tumble about on a dizzy, swimming earthscape, losing all sense of direction.

An invisible force now pushes you down through a narrow passage where you can no longer feel wandering spirits or hear their inner ravings. You can only hear the drum of silence, but through this uninterrupted silence you can make out the magick and listen to the secrets:

"Seeker, to solve this ancient puzzle, for it is the puzzle of the labyrinth, anti-clockwise you must venture to unwind all that you know." Is this the voice of truth? You ask yourself as yet more passageways present themselves, most of them leading to an abrupt end.

It seems like an eternity as you wander along, feeling your way through this maze. On the walls of these passages are carvings of the forty-two daemons, creatures with heads of snakes, vultures, hawks, and rams, and each one holds a knife! You quickly jerk your hand away for fear of awakening them, but they know of your presence as you can hear their soft groans.

You finally reach the centre. Very sleepy, you lie down on a bed of silence on an island surrounded by black flames, the flames of eternity, in the middle of this ancient labyrinth.

Around you, the violet-scented air seems to split in two like a torn curtain as the great lord Sobek appears before you. His reptilian head doesn't seem at all strange on the body of a man.

Proud and regal, this god stands holding the uwas sceptre in Set's likeness.

"Ask of me all you search for, but speak in riddles, speak in my tongue lest all others hear."

As if you have always done so, you automatically utter soul sounds in the ancient tongue of Sobek. Pictures flash before you, each appearing in a separate chamber, and each one has its own meaning. Many thousands of names are written, and you learn the names and all their secrets; you learn all the medicine, charms of magick, and how to use them.

As Set touched you in the Setereion, so does Sobek in his labyrinth with a touch as light as a feather being passed across your face. He speaks in a booming voice that echoes throughout the centre of his labyrinth, into the passageways, into all the three thousand rooms and beyond for all to hear. He has uttered his decree which none shall dare countermand. "It is done, pilgrim."

Then, from the land of sleep and silence, you awake from your dream state; clockwise you retrace your footsteps. Along winding pathways forward and along darkened corridors that house shadowy forms, you walk tall and proud. From out of the darkness of fear and ignorance you have emerged triumphant, changed forever!

This time you hear whispers of a different kind. They are the lost souls crying from their darkness; all were fated to wander down there in the maze of the labyrinth forever. Are they the seekers who did not make the journey? Each one is pleading, "Take me with you, take me with you."

But these are really your discarded thoughts, and worn out memories of a previous life, of a death, and now a rebirth. Onwards and upwards you go, out of chaos and confusion and into a world of harmony and order, of mind and emotions.

As you exit the great mastaba, Djehuty is there to greet you. But it is a different greeting.

"I honour you, Seeker of the Mysteries," he says, bowing low.

You stand taller in the fading light of Ra near the shadow of the mastaba that houses the fearful labyrinth. It was a great testing for you in the inner sanctum of the heartland of Sobek. The old guardian steps forward and, bowing low to you, explains:

"Your mind is likened to this labyrinth, like a many-roomed palace. Many seekers have faced their limits and have visited only just a few rooms, leaving the rest in total darkness. And those rooms they chose to visit, only a few windows were ever opened, leaving the rest in total darkness; this is likened to the darkness and ignorance of the mind.

"You have been to all these rooms in your mind and in the maze and have awakened your senses to question everything. You see, my dear Seeker, the only evil that exists is the evil of ignorance."

So a mind is likened to the many-roomed labyrinth. What the old guardian said to you may almost be beyond your comprehension. But on reflection, you do feel different. You have challenged and have been challenged, and in a way, you are the victor.

Now construct and visualise your pylons and walk through the portal to your world of familiar regions. Utter your secret name to the gods and seal the door behind you.

SIXTEEN

LEGEND OF PTAH

I (Ramses III) made for thee (Ptah) a mysterious shrine
of Elephantine granite, established with work forever,
of a single block, having double doors of bronze, of a mixture of six
(parts), engraved with thy august name, forever.

PAPYRUS HARRIS

Ptah was the ancient creator god in Memphite creation myth, whose name may have meant "the opener" or "sculptor." He was associated with two other ancient Memphite deities, Ta-Tenen, an earth god, and Sokar, god of the necropolis, whose attributes were absorbed in early times. As a result, Ptah manifested as Ptah-Ta-Tenen and Ptah-Sokar, which in later times metamorphosed into Ptah-Sokar-Osiris.

From his very beginnings he has appeared in human form, shrouded like a mummy, hands projecting from wrappings to hold a sceptre composed of the uwas (dominion), djed (stability), and the ankh (life). Sometimes he held the crook and flail and always wore a wedge-shaped beard and close-fitting skullcap, with the shoulders covered by a broad collar with a counterpoise called a menat, which hung from the base of his neck.

In addition to the mummiform appearance, he has two epithets which are quite specific to him, Ptah "Res Inebef," "Ptah Who is South of His Wall," referring to the boundary wall which enclosed the precinct in his temple at Men-nefer; and Ptah "Nefer-her,"

"Ptah, Beautiful of Face," referring to the splendour of his divine being, the only part of him which was visible apart from his hands.

At this stage, we have to ask ourselves what lies at the heart of this Neter, behind the beautifully serene composure. For further clues it may be useful to carefully scrutinise the Memphite creation theology; much that is hidden lore may be gleaned from its concepts and your own creative impulses. It was inscribed upon a piece of black basalt, known as the Shabaka Stone, commissioned by King Shabaka with the purpose of preserving an ancient text that was said to have been written on papyrus recounting the creation of life by Ptah.

The inscriptions relate to a time in the very beginning when nothingness reigned until Ptah thought the Universe into being, a deity containing many other deities within himself. Through effort of heart (the seat of his intellect) and tongue (command to action) did he create life, commanding the great lord of time and wisdom, Djehuty, to put his wishes into action. This displays a marked deviation from the more earthy account of Atum masturbating into his hand to create life! Memphite theology contains within it concepts which would appeal to the more mystically and intellectually minded individual.

When it was discovered in the nineteenth century, the archaeologist found that the Shabaka Stone had been used as a millstone. On closer inspection, he realised that the partly obliterated text down each side was attributed to a far earlier time than the eighth century BCE.

Ptah's relationship with Men-nefer (Memphis) or Ineb-hedj, "the City of the White Wall," was established early in the city's conception and the unification of the Two Lands. As his influence soon spread throughout Khemit, he took on the mantle of state deity. Men-nefer's prominence rose and fell over the ages, as did the cult of Ptah, but both retained their importance throughout the long history of ancient Khemit.

At the height of its power, the "Balance of the Two Lands" (Men-nefer) ushered in a period of incredible creativity, blessed by the beneficence of its patron deity. Ptah was revered by craftsmen and artisans and was thought to be the Divine Craftsman and Architect of the Universe. As a creator god, he shaped both human and divine beings, vivifying them through the divine breath.

Indeed, his high priests were given the title of "wer kherep hemw" (supreme leader of craftsmen) and held responsibility for overseeing the operations of the numerous craftsmen who were engaged in perpetuating the superb artistic legacy evident in ancient Egyptian culture. Thus did they carry out the decrees of the living god, Pharaoh, for the glory of his divine father. (The fact that these individuals were drawn from a powerful ruling elite who were close to the throne did little harm.)

The city had a number of shrines and temples dedicated to many deities, but the Temple of Ptah was considered the most important, with successive pharaohs lavishing both time and money over it. Ptah's temple was given the appellation "the Mansion of the Soul of Ptah" (Hwt-Ka-Pth), which was in later days taken by the Greeks as the name for the whole of Khemit—"Ai-gy-ptos." As chief deity, he ruled over Men-nefer with his consort Sekhmet and their child, Nefertum.

The temple now lies buried beneath the modern village of Mit-Rahina, its magnificence lost to the passage of time and just a ghostly memory, on the earthy plane that is, but its white walls gleaming for all eternity on another plane, waiting. As does its main deity, Ptah, watching and waiting for a time when humanity will open itself to the higher knowledge he is custodian of.

Before you proceed further, pilgrim, ponder upon what this PATH (PTAH) means to you…mark it well. What is it that you wish to put into action on this earthly plane? What is it that you wish to create and what will you do with such creations? Your thoughts have power, your words have power—use both with discernment and discrimination. This mysterious and awesome Neter watches you intently from the First Time, and he knows that which lies slumbering within yourself, as well he should do with his creation.

Ptah was thought to have created the ritual of the Opening of Mouth Ceremony, which was performed on the mummified corpse and statues of the deceased and gods. It was an important ritual used in both funerary and temple practices and you shall partake in this sacred ceremony on this path.

PATH TO PTAH
Journey to Ineb-hedj

Don your white robe and tie blue and purple cords around your waist. This will be in respect of the Neter you will be working with.

Build your pylons and make the sign of the ankh in the air above your head. On the lintel of the portal, hieroglyphs of Ptah appear.

Commit them to memory. These symbols are charged; look at each mark and take it within. As you utter your secret name your journey takes you to Ineb-hedj, "the City of the White Wall," ancient capital of the Two Lands where you will commune with the god Ptah. This is a gateway that will take you to the heart of his realm. You will learn how to focus on his energy as you are drawn in.

You emerge into a landscape that is strangely recognisable. The light is sharper and brighter than previously experienced. There is a potent energy here and the magick literally crackles and sparkles in the air. You breathe in this essence and, as it flows through your body, it subtly changes form, reawakening ancient memories that have slumbered in your cells. It is a call from a time when the Neters were manifest on earth, from a time when they walked with humankind and were not just memories. *They lived*!

"You can feel it, can you not?" a voice whispers in your ear. Without turning around, you know it is your guardian. A smile crosses your lips. Your heart swells with vitality and life. Yes, the atmosphere evokes primeval energies resonating from Khemit's youth.

Djehuty sighs as he surveys the scene before him and, in a low undertone, he begins to murmur a spell. A shape takes form from the haze of the desert sun; little by little it solidifies into dazzling white walls that shimmer and glow in such wondrous beauty; Ineb-hedj is before you. These walls seem to stretch for miles as you gaze at the city with disbelief.

"It is magnificent," you gasp.

"The Balance of the Two Lands," Djehuty utters. "All who gazed upon it did not remain untouched by its splendour. It held all our hopes and desires, yet to gaze upon it as it is in your time sorely grieves my heart. It was a star within the firmament of Khemit's heavenly environs."

He turns to look at you intently; something stirs within the depths of his eyes. Sorrow fleetingly moves its shadows across his face.

"What sights has he been privy to?" you wonder. Silently he proffers a hand and you grasp it without hesitation.

Both of you make your way towards the city gates that open silently at your approach. The energy within the city walls feels different, in some way a space set apart. Whatever it is makes your body tingle. The eerie emptiness does much to heighten the air of mystery. Then a movement catches your attention. Shapes emerge from the shadows but they are as insubstantial as the breath of the wind. Shimmering energy forms flow past and through you.

Sound then breaks the silence as the chattering of voices assails your ears.

Djehuty explains that Ineb-hedj still exists in another dimension but is lost to our ordinary senses. Lost that is to the unillumined, but not to the Seeker, whose heart is filled with purity and love. It is then that true sight pierces the veils of illusion.

Djehuty walks at an unhurried pace, letting you take your time absorbing the atmosphere. His silence conveys much and you find your mind is filled with a myriad of images, symbols, and emotions. Your conscious mind can make no sense of this communication but within the shadowy depths of the psyche something stirs in recognition. The feeling grows in intensity as you find yourself standing before the original temple enclosure.

The complex is entered through a further gateway flanked by two large poles topped with banners. You notice it is oval in shape with the shrine positioned to the rear of the enclosure. In the centre of the courtyard is a larger pole topped with the city's sepat, the nome standard.

The shrine itself is a structure composed of reed matting attached to a wooden framework. It is built from simple materials that are artfully shaped to convey majesty and awe. Grouped around the shrine are the workshops of the temple craftsmen. To think such places were prototypes for the massive temples of later millennia is astonishing.

Your musings are interrupted by a soft but penetrating voice that draws you towards the shrine. You glance at Djehuty questioningly but he gives nothing away, only to briefly say:

"Go, your heart and mind will it. He awaits you."

Gathering up your courage, you make your way towards the entrance of the shrine to be met by a priest who has been standing there for some time, assessing you. Djehuty silently hands you over into his care and you are led over the threshold into the sanctum. The interior gloom is illuminated only by a few simple lamps that cast strange shadows onto the woven walls. The scent of carnation, frankincense, and myrrh hangs heavy in the air; it makes your head spin, but that could be the intensity of power concentrated within this place. The divine is truly present here. You can feel it in every vibration, every thought; every feeling causes your heart to beat loudly, so loudly that it drowns out every other sound, or so you think!

Ptah stands at the back of the shrine enveloped in shadow. The lamp flickers, causing him to suddenly emerge. He is indeed glorious, robed in a garment of golden serpentine-like scales. He wears a turquoise blue skullcap framing a face beyond youth and age. Such calm and beauty radiate from him, fittingly he was called Ptah Nefer-Her, "Ptah, Beautiful of Face." Piercing bright jewel-green eyes burn deep into your soul. He knows all and sees all, so there is nowhere to hide, no subterfuge which can be entered into. Your innermost essence is laid bare.

He speaks and the sound envelops every single atom of your being. You feel as if you have been thrust into the very heart of the Universe, sleeping and waiting, waiting for the call to come into existence. Your voice is silent and as such unawakened to consciousness. He knows what you seek and knows your true self can offer that most sacred of gifts.

Ptah utters that which is hidden within your heart, gives it life and breath. Prepared are you thus for the sacred ritual that has been enacted since the Sacred Mound rose from the waters of chaos—the Opening of Mouth Ceremony.

Djehuty materialises beside you, as do several priests to take you to the place of purification. The walls and roof of the shrine dissolve into nothingness and you find yourself standing on a golden knoll with gently sloping sides that vanish into the endless waters of Nun.

Behind you is the reed shrine and above, endless skies. There is nothing on the horizon. All is silent. Then a voice flows across the waters and wraps itself around all who stand on the Primeval Mound. It contains the sum of all that exists and will exist. Force takes form and the Divine Artificer stands before you in all his splendour. Now it begins, the journey into full consciousness.

Priests gather round you, wrapping you like a mummy in pristine white linen. Wahabs intone the sacred vowel sounds, their voices radiating out into the eternal silence beyond. Incense of quema is wafted around you.

Symbolic sacrifices are made ready and presented to you in the form of a heart and foreleg of a bull, and a head of duck and an antelope. In these ancient times, they needed blood and flesh sacrifices. A Kher-heb utters:

"For Temu, I have seized them and I present them to the Seeker."

Djehuty whispers:

"You are no stranger to this ritual; you are remembering this old practice."

In the shadows of this ancient chamber lurks a covered form of pure mystery. Ever quiet, ever present, and ever watchful hides the figure of the Tekenu wrapped in Mesca. He represents the sacred Ka sign, and like a doorway, the Tekenu will open the path for your soul to pass through as it retains its rebirth. Like Ra passing through Nut's body every evening as he rests, so the Ka performs its duty.

Mighty Ptah steps forward and thus begins the process of unveiling and revivifying.

"With sacred adze, I free your mouth so that breath and utterances may flow forth."

"With Seb-Hur, mighty instrument of Anpu, I open your eyes so that the divine within may gaze upon the world and the light of consciousness pierce the mighty halls of the temple within."

Once more you are censed with the quema from far Nekhen.

The Kher-heb steps forward, saying:

"Thou art pure; may you receive the golden Ur-Hekau charged with the might of Ophidian current."

The Sem Priest addresses you, saying:

"With the might of the Neter, I open your mouth with the sacred Smu."

Behind you now stands the Sem Priest, who places Meshenti on your head, the regal crown, whilst the Kher-heb incenses your forehead with natron.

Thus is the sacred centre upon your forehead illumined. Four boxes of purification are pressed upon your mouth and eyes.

The Pesh-en-Kef, sacred tool of Set, is placed upon your jaw-bone and grapes are offered to you. Ptah utters:

"May these fruits be the power words of wisdom."

The Tun-tet of ostrich feather is wafted over your head by the Sem Priest, who says:

"May the roads be open to you."

A final order is given to the wahabs who remove the linen bindings from your body. You are then dressed in fine raiment. The nemes collar is placed around your neck, representing the symbol of light of Nekheb; your eyes are then painted with finest metchem and oil of u-atch. Khyphi incense wafts around you and, with his hands extended, the Sem Priest recites the blessings:

"Sesenet neftu nedjem,
Per em rek,
Per Neteri nefruk em menet,
Ta-I nehet sedj emi,
Kheruk nedjem en mehit,
Rnpu ha-I em ankh,
En mituk."

"May you breathe the sweet breath,
That comes forth from thy mouth,
That we behold your beauty every day,
It is our desire that you
May be rejuvenated with life
Through love of thee."

The life force grows stronger within you and the brilliance of the Creator's light fills every single cell of your being. Ptah the Holy One then utters:

"You have been renewed and exist within eternity. Neither time nor age shall affect you, neither worldly matters corrupt you, nor evil forces obliterate you. I have freed you from the limitations of the material world so that you shall rise above it and reach out to the stars. Perceive this world as it really is and not as you believe it to be. You have passed the threshold of this reality and expanded your consciousness. Within, you have the keys to the universal Mysteries; guard them well. My breath have I given you, and my heart."

Your guardian appears by your side and murmurs:

"The gates of our hearts have been opened up to you. What will you do with such knowledge?"

Silence is the road you take. There is no need for words; you know the answer. To have come this far upon this journey without faltering is answer enough. All fades and you find yourself back within the reed shrine. This too melts into the air and you find yourself outside the city walls. Djehuty lays a comforting arm upon your shoulders as he leads you back to the portal. This is not a time for words but for inward contemplation. You utter your secret name and find yourself back in present time.

SEVENTEEN

LEGEND OF DJEHUTY

I am Thoth, the skilled scribe whose hands are pure,
A possessor of purity, who drives away evil, who
Writes what is true, who detests falsehood, whose pen
Defends the Lord of All.

BOOK OF THE DEAD

He was known by many names—Thoth, Thot, Tehuty, Tahuti—
but throughout this book, we have called him by his correct
name, Djehuty.

He was one of the earliest Egyptian Neters and was thought
to have been a scribe to the gods and keeper of a great library of
scrolls, over which one of his wives, Seshat, was the goddess of
writing.

According to legend he created the five extra days, known as
"epagomenal" days, from the lunar timings to make up the full 365
days of the year. He was also called "Reckoner of Years," his attributes being a writing tablet and palm-leaf stylus. He was protector of scribes, teachers, writers, mathematicians, speech, and art;
in fact, Djehuty was patron Neter to everyone who disseminated
knowledge.

He was a measurer and recorder of time, as was Seshat, who
was believed to be the author of the spells in the Sacred Book of
Per-t em hru, commonly known as the Book of the Dead.

Djehuty was both helper and punisher of the deceased as they tried to enter the underworld. In this role, his other wife was the goddess Ma'at, the personification of order, whose symbol, the feather, was weighed against the heart of the dead to see if they followed *ma'at*, truth, during their life.

Djehuty was usually depicted as an ibis-headed man or as a full ibis, or with the face of a dog-headed baboon and the body of a man or, again, as a full dog-headed baboon. The ibis, it is thought, had a crescent-shaped beak, linking the bird to the moon. The dog-headed baboon, on the other hand, was seen by the Egyptians as a night animal who would greet the sun each morning with chattering noises just as Djehuty, the moon god, would greet Ra, the sun god, as he rose. He was also associated with the tongue and heart of Ra.

There were two paths of training in the temple at Khemenu. The first was the Path of Wisdom where Djehuty was considered the supreme Neter of wisdom, intelligence, and knowledge. Wisdom was not just an abstract belief but also a working ethical understanding. The underlying principle in ancient Egypt was to develop each individual person to his highest potential. The Path of Wisdom was not only training of the person but a renaissance of his birth.

The second was the Path of Ritual Magick that included training in all forms of divination, astrology, healing, and setep-sa, meaning "to make passes." Priests on this path would aid the transmission of the Sa to the king from the statue of the god by means of placing the arms of the statue round the king, and laying one of its hands on the nape of his neck as he knelt before it.

Since there was always a shrine to Ma'at on this temple site, it made sense that many of the judges, and all of the well-known viziers, were priests of this Neter and would have undergone their training in Khemenu.

PATH TO DJEHUTY
Journey to Khemenu

Don your white robe and tie a blue cord around your waist. This will be in respect of the Neter you will be working with.

Build your pylons and make the sign of the ankh in the air above your head. On the lintel of the portal, hieroglyphs of Djehuty appear:

Commit them to memory. These symbols are charged; look at each mark and take it within. As you utter your secret name, your journey takes you to Khemenu, the heart of Djehuty's realm. You will learn how to focus on his energy as you are drawn in.

The moon has just risen, but the west is still full of colour and light, then it fades and is replaced by silver moonbeams that fall upon the entrance of a magnificent gate. In front of this grand entrance stand two red granite obelisks, flanked by a pair of ram-headed sphinxes and two colossal statues of Pharaoh Rameses II. A tall man walks toward you. His head is shaven and oiled. He is dressed in a pleated white linen kilt; his palm-leafed sandals are edged with gold. A collar of gold circles his strong neck. Draped over his left shoulder and falling down his back hangs the leopard skin of the Sem Priest. He bows his head slightly and says:

"I am Ta-em Hotep, Sem Priest in my lord Djehuty's temple. I welcome you to Khemenu."

You follow him through the gateway into a colonnaded courtyard where the priests of the temple have assembled. You pause to watch them. Even though they are all dressed in the same long white linen kilts, there is an air of subtlety, combined with a pure simplicity and sense of mystery about each one of them.

They slowly begin to make their way to the sanctuary for evening prayers. But it is not this place you will be led to; it is to a mighty white tower surrounded by a garden. Just beyond it is the sacred lake upon which float the sleeping lotuses that have closed and will not reopen until Ra rises the next morning. The sounds of croaking frogs, crickets, and singing birds drift across the gardens.

You want to ask where your guardian is, but the priest looks at you with a glint in his eyes and puts his finger to his lips, indicating silence.

You follow the Sem Priest to Djehuty's special sanctum, high above the roof of the temple. At the bottom of the tower, the priest bids you farewell and you begin your long climb up mudbrick stairs that lead to the roof. You are surprised to see that the walls of the tower are crumbling and fast returning to the dust from whence they came.

You reach the rooftop. By now the moon is high in the heavens and shrouded within Nut's starry form; only a bar of dull red hangs in the western sky where Ra has sunk. Minutes of silent expectation pass, while the moon waxes stronger and sends a cascade of silver onto the temple below.

A dark shape is moving in the sky above you, black against the afterglow of the sunset, that makes you feel uneasy. The air is filled with camphor, myrrh, violet, and musk. Suddenly the flapping of wings swirls around you. You want to retreat back down the stairs but the bird-form bars your way. It is Djehuty in his guise as the ibis. You are not sure if you like to see him this way, finding it difficult to communicate with a bird.

He senses this and resumes his human form, saying:

"Here on this special night you will embark upon a road that will change your life forever. Seeker of the Mysteries, I have observed you as you have walked the many paths to be with my fellow Neters. I have watched you grow and change. I will now share a very special secret, the secret of all being, the secret of the world!"

With a grand gesture he raises his hands to the heavens, and in a clear voice utters the first spell:

"I Djehuty, keeper of the letters, lord of time, of all being, reveal to me the mysteries of the heavens and all the earth from the mountains to the seas. Reveal to me the language of every beast and bird and give me the power to summon the scaled ones of the deep."

At first nothing happens. A deadly silence gathers about you, the trees in the temple gardens cease to stir, the birds stop their evening song, frogs and crickets are silent. It is as if all life has been snuffed out.

Then it happens. The very substance of matter collapses around you as the walls of the tower are being pulled sideways at varying speeds, and beneath your feet a huge chasm opens up. You grip the sides of the walls in terror and struggle to focus on the events occurring around you. Gases belch forth, followed by brilliant flashes of white light that now fill the void. You are afraid of what is happening around you.

From within the smouldering mass that is now forming, great mountains of rock push their way up towards the murkiness of what appears to be the heavens. Then the sky opens and pours forth more than the tears of Isis. Great torrents now fall earthward, filling up valleys, producing vast stretches of water that go on and on for as far as you can see.

Djehuty is still very much in charge and continues to conduct this orchestra of chaos.

Within the watery mass swim fish of all sizes, whilst around you roam the beasts of the earth in search of food. Birds of all kinds fly above your head. Throughout all this chaos, an order is slowly forming and the cacophony of sounds about you now becomes a language you understand, and you cry with joy that pleases Djehuty to no end.

"I now have power over the fish of the seas and the beasts of the field," he cries, and with a deep intake of breath he utters the second spell:

"I Djehuty, reveal to me the mystery of Nut giving birth to the stars. Show me the rising and setting of the great god Ra, then let me see the true faces of all the gods themselves. Give me the tongue so that I may speak to them as one god to another."

Again all becomes quiet. After a further movement in the heavens, a sudden red flush stains the sky that is neither light nor gas but more a great presence. A host of inner voices begin speaking to Djehuty in many tongues. They surround him with such euphoria, making the great god swoon with pleasure. Then about him appears a god-form so large it makes you stagger backwards in shock; Nut's blue body stretches backwards in such contortions, sending great ripples throughout the cosmos. The ripples then turn into the music of the spheres that only the gods can hear. You begin to tune in to their wondrous sounds.

Slowly the stars around Nut's heavenly body begin to fade and, with a further burst of sound that almost shatters your eardrums, Ra appears in all of his godlike forms, allowing you to see him and feel his essence. Ra touches your forehead with his left index finger. Never have you felt such trust, blessing, courage, rebirth, mystery, truth, and wisdom. Each time Ra speaks, your body resonates to his voice, charging it with the power of remembering that has laid dormant for millennia. Within this magickal realm you see the faces of all the gods and goddesses, each one visiting you in turn, touching your forehead.

You close your eyes as if in a dream, and when you open them, you are sitting by the sacred lake with Djehuty by your side. You look up at the sky where all is quiet and full of crystal coldness. What you have witnessed was the absolute magick of Djehuty—that which was written upon his scroll and you recall the words:

"These symbols are for my eyes only, or for one who is pure enough to read these signs and not use them for their own pur-

pose." Although you were not privy to the scroll, you were captivated and held for a moment in time by this god's magick. Again
you want to say something to Djehuty but he touches your forehead, bestowing a blessing. Thus does he transmit his holy words
to you for all time. Be content in the knowledge that these sacred
symbols are now in your safekeeping for all eternity.

Alas, it is time to leave his realm. You feel both elation and
exhaustion as you construct your pylons and walk through the
portal to your world of familiar regions. Utter your secret name to
the gods and seal the door behind you.

EIGHTEEN

LEGEND OF TEFNUT AND SHU

Then Shu and Tefnut rejoiced from out of the inert watery mass wherein they and I were, and they brought to me my Eye (Ra).

E. A. WALLIS BUDGE, *LEGENDS OF THE EGYPTIAN GODS*

According to the Heliopolitan creation myth, Shu and Tefnut were the first couple to be fashioned by the creator god Atum when he either masturbated or expectorated, producing new life that he then split into opposites. In the version of the myth where Atum spits out the deities, Shu being formed from the breath of Atum becomes the god of air and essentially life itself (his name probably means "He who rises up"); and his sister-wife, Tefnut, being formed from the mucus, becomes the goddess of moisture or damp, corrosive air.

After their birth they wander off into the depths of Nun, instigating Atum to send his Eye to recover his children. Once they are found, Atum names Shu "Life" and Tefnut "Order," being personifications of natural forces. Shu and Tefnut mate producing Geb, the earth god, and Nut, the sky goddess. Thus are created the first elements of life, but the creative process is not yet complete until earth has been separated from sky. Sky and earth are found in an eternal embrace, and in order for life to begin, Shu has to separate his daughter Nut from her lover Geb. Nut is held aloft whilst Geb is held supine on the ground.

Shu is usually portrayed in human form wearing a plume on his head, either kneeling or standing with arms raised, supporting the heavens. Even though he was a god of sunlight, Shu was not considered to be a solar deity. The solar connection was attributed because of his act of raising the sun in the sky, and accordingly bringing Ra (and the pharaoh) to life each morning. He was one of the gods who protected Ra on his journey through the underworld by using magick spells to ward off Ra's enemy, the underworld snake god Apophis. As with other protector gods, Shu had a darker side—he was also a god of punishment in the land of the dead, leading executioners and torturers to kill off the corrupt souls.

Tefnut is generally shown as a woman with a lion's head wearing the solar disk and uraeus, and holding a sceptre and the ankh. She is also portrayed as a full lioness. Being related to moisture, Tefnut was also linked to the moon and was originally thought to be the lunar "Eye of Ra" and linked to the night sky, as well as dew, rain, and mist. Tefnut's lunar attributions change over time to the solar aspect and she becomes known as an "Eye of Ra," so joining the ranks of Bast, Sekhmet, Hathor, Wadjet, and Nekhbet.

As an "Eye of Ra," Tefnut displays the destructive aspects of the sun upon the land of Khemit when she flees into Nubia, taking all the moisture and water with her. In a fit of anger against Ra, she embarks upon a killing spree, almost wiping out humanity. It is only through the intervention of Djehuty and Shu that a disaster is averted and the goddess is brought back to Khemit. This story explains how the goddess of moisture could also be the goddess of dryness, heat, and the negative aspects of the sun. The people believed that without her water, Egypt could dry and burn in the sun. So she took on the form of a lion, as did the other goddesses with the "Eye of Ra" title, and was also strongly linked to the sun.

Shu and Tefnut shared a sanctuary in the Delta at Nay-ta-hut (Leontopolis of the Greeks) and were worshipped in the form of two lions who guarded the eastern and western horizons. The lion of the eastern horizon watched over the rising of the sun each morning and the lion of the western horizon guarded the sun by night. The association of lions with the two horizons may have become linked because of lions being found living on the desert margins and, over time, becoming regarded as guardians of the places where sunrise and sunset occurred. The Egyptians visualized a universal mountain split into a western peak (Manu) and an eastern peak (Bakhu), which served as the supports for heaven.

These animals sometimes replaced the eastern and western mountains, symbols of both past and future, on either side of the horizon (akhet) hieroglyph. Headrests took the form of the akhet symbol supported by two lions. As the sun was born each morning and died each evening on the horizons, the lion was also connected with death and rebirth.

PATH TO TEFNUT AND SHU
Journey to Giza

Don your white robe and tie blue and white cords around your waist. This will be in respect of the Neters you will be working with.

Build your pylons and make the sign of the ankh in the air above your head. On the lintel of the portal, hieroglyphs of Tefnut and Shu appear:

Commit them to memory. This symbol is charged; look at each mark and take it within. As you utter your secret name, your journey takes you to the plains of Giza where you will commune with the gods Tefnut and Shu. This is a gateway that will take you to the heart of their realm. You will learn how to focus on their energy as you are drawn in.

On a moonlit night you arrive at Giza. Khemenu is far behind you but your experience in your guardian's realm lingers long in your memory. It has profoundly changed your perception of reality and understanding of Self. All that is extraneous has been cleared from your consciousness and now only the road towards further enlightenment lies before you. You look up at the skies and wonder what slumbers within its vast and velvety darkness.

Above you shine Merek and Duhbe, stars from the constellation of Ursa Major. Djehuty materialises next to you and stands also looking up at the stars, and says:

"We call these stars Mesxet. Come, let us venture to Rostau, one of the many hidden gateways to the world beyond."

Before you sits the eternal Great Sphinx, within him locked all the mystery of his being, all his mystery and his magick, all his beauty in his spirit. You gaze upward at this wonder in moonlight, and you ask yourself:

"Why sits this creature all alone on this plateau in the company of twin chapels?'

Djehuty looks wisely at you, having read your thoughts, and replies:

"Why the twin chapels? They are the brothers Heru-Sutekh. You have touched upon the oldest mystery, when here in my land of Khemit, we had an Age of Twinning."

With the backdrop of the lonely Sphinx and the star-studded body of Nut above, Djehuty utters:

"Re nu per-t em hru! We call upon Manu and Bakhet, summits of the two horizons. I summon thee to show thyself to the Seeker!"

From the eyelids of the sunrise, a holy light shines on the face of the Sphinx, but it is not the human face of a long-dead pharaoh you see, but the divine lion head of Shu in all his glory, and with a voice so pure he cries:

"In the east I am Sut the Opener, I am Tomorrow, the one called Heru-Khuti at the dawning, and as Ra travels across the noonday sky he becomes Re-Heru-Khuti. At the close of day, Ra caresses my sister Tefnut."

With these words the landscape around you changes; a flaming, glistening red spreads across the horizon as Ra makes his last journey across the heavens towards the portals of Nut. A great rift appears in the earth, and beside Shu appears out of the sands of time yet another lion-headed sphinx, his sister Tefnut. The breathtaking tints fall upon her yellow body, and you hear her call out, saying:

"In the west I am Heru the closer, she of Yesterday. I allow the rays of Ra to shine upon my body as he turns into Temu-Heru-Khuti."

As the dying light falls, and against the opalescent background, you see the twins as they once were, all those millennia ago. Elements of air and water, born of air sailing eastward and floating on the waters westward, Shu and Tefnut are side by side. Shu turns his head wistfully, looking back on the days when he could always count on her being with him.

"Ah, but now she can only visit me when summoned by the mighty Djehuty." Too brief, too brief.

The aroma of wisterias and camphor fill the air around you as the twins are reunited once more.

Ra now commences again his nightly journey from west to east. He travels to the underworld as Temu-Heru-Khuti rests in the womb of Nut. In the morning he will be reborn from the stellar mother as Heru-Khuti. You watch the mystery as Djehuty explains:

"Nut is mother to the solar as she swallows her sun child Heru, and gives birth to her stellar son, Sutekh.

"At the dawn of our beginning, the heavens were much closer to earth, and we the Neters were more familiar with man. Underneath the Sphinx of Tefnut in the west holds the entire history of Zep Tepi, where once we were able to cross the abyss to create reality. In those days we could walk the land between heaven and earth."

You look wide-eyed at Djehuty and yearn to ask the question:

"Have you keys that hold a secret?"

"Ah yes," Djehuty answers, "but they are not keys: one has to utter sacred sounds. They are multilayered sound forms that pass you through to a third dimension and onto other planes of notions, onto other spheres of being, to the greater and the higher."

You bravely ask:

"May I utter then these soul sounds?"

Djehuty shakes his head, saying:

"There'll come another time of reason, when all mankind is ripe and ready, when his pineal gland opens; only then will these hidden chambers reveal past memory. Man will profit with this knowledge, thus linking him with his maker, linking his past with his future, linking terra with the stellar."

As you gaze upon the face and body of Tefnut, longing for the day that will reveal all to you, you detect a movement in the stone. Are her eyes looking at you, or is that her giant cat's tail switching through the sand? And is that a hint of peppermint you can smell? Then she disappears as suddenly as she came into your vista. A great wind begins to blow, stirring your robe; only the linen kilt of Djehuty does not stir. He stands as a sentinel at the gates of time and space itself, inscrutable and all-powerful. Eyes that have gazed upon these first beings at the start of creation pierce the veils of existence. The Great Lord of Time calls for his kin and they answer; in response, a vortex builds around you both. They commune, but you know not of what they speak. Their words are cloaked in silence.

For once on this journey, you, the pilgrim, feel as if you are an outsider. There is much you are still not privy to, but it will be revealed as your spiritual evolution progresses. "Have patience," a voice whispers in your ear. Patience? You understand it must be so but your heart grieves sorely. How long must humanity wait before it progresses to the next stage of its evolution and the lost knowledge is regained?

Djehuty looks so sad and, shaking his head, takes you gently by your arm and leads you to the remaining sphinx, holding himself ever aloof, almost like the soul of man that can retreat at will. You think to yourself:

"So, if we have a past, then we must have a future?" Djehuty nods in agreement, and gesturing to this lone creature in stone he says:

"In this Great Sphinx that faces eastward were dug in ancient times shallow caverns. They were never marked with symbols; the cavern was left void; a promised future.

"But, then came the Greek regals who made inscriptions on the sandstone walls. But they wrote nothing of any importance. There were no words of a promised future; their words were empty-prided notions. As they did not stem from any royal-blood pharaohs, they had learned nothing from the glorious past of Khemit. Little did they understand of our sacred teachings and even less understanding did they have of my divine brethren. We were as fanciful creatures garbed in unfamiliar robes, speaking in strange tongues. Just mere apparitions."

Djehuty senses that you are anxious to know more about the sphinx in the west and says:

"On the right side of Shu was his sister Tefnut. Now she is gone, like her past time. But her secret chambers are hidden, still waiting to be reopened. Alas, you mortals will have to wait. This time is not far off. You are on a journey moving ever closer. Night by night the sands of time are shifting. Closer are you to the real truth, as you move away from stasis through a time of chaos, and into the everlasting divine order of things."

The lone sphinx has gradually taken possession of you, so gradually you have learned to feel his majesty and magickal mystery that has reigned on this plateau from the beginning of time. As you walk away from him, with his false head and beard of a vain pharaoh, you will return and know the secrets from within. The golden rays of Ra rise and tenderly kiss the remnants of his lion in the east. Such is the passion amongst the Neters.

It is time for you to leave Rostau. Now construct your pylons and walk through the portal to your world of familiar regions. Utter your secret name to the gods and seal the door behind you. You will return.

The Pyramid of Khufu awaits you!

NINETEEN

LEGEND OF SET AND HORUS

*There came to pass the testing of Horus and Seth,
mysterious in (their) forms and mightiest of the princes
and magnates who (ever) came into existence.*

CHESTER BEATTY PAPYRUS

For centuries, since the Great Pyramid's chambers have been opened
to the many visitors, throughout the ages archaeologists and Egyp-
tologists have confused everyone with false notions of some fantastic burial place for the long-deceased King Khufu.

Since no evidence has been discovered to support this idea of
a final resting place for the king, I put it to you that the so-called
King's and Queen's Chambers were used for another, and more
significant, purpose other than burial.

We must first look at the ritual of the Heb Sed festival of renewal, and rebirth of the pharaoh. This highly charged event
would take place every thirty years of the king's reign, but in
some of the earlier dynasties, it was celebrated more frequently.

The king would run in the open space between the two rows
of shrines dressed alternatively in the insignia colours of white
for Upper, and red for Lower Egypt. This ritual race around the
"field" was repeated four times as the ruler of the south, and four
times as ruler of the north.

This was indeed a very public occasion, witnessed by Pharaoh's subjects who not only regarded this as a great spectacle, but also put great store in the safe delivery of their king as he ran the gamut.

But the true test of Pharaoh's strength was not to be physical. This test was indeed an act of rebirth and renewal of mind and spirit, and the ritual setting would have been the great pyramid of Khufu.

The king would be prepared in the usual manner in his stately regalia, and together with a retinue of priests and attendees, he would make his way from the valley of the Great Sphinx, up the flag-stoned causeway, to the entrance of the Great Pyramid.

Pharaoh would then be relieved of his cape, sceptres, and crowns, and remained dressed only in a short white linen kilt. After priestly blessings, he would then venture alone, through the pyramid entrance bearing the hieroglyph letter of the god Hapy, and into the dimly lit corridor of the pyramid.

If we look at a cross-section of the Great Pyramid of Khufu, we will notice that the passageways and shafts leading to the two chambers resemble the constellation of Ursa Major. We must also look at the corresponding link between the shape of the adze, fashioned out of tektites that were painstakingly gathered from the surrounding desert, and were later smelted down to make this instrument.

As Pharaoh made his way up through the pyramid, he would then be reduced to the very form of the constellation of the Plough, which is also representative of the god Set. In this doubling, crawling, and walking phase, the king proceeds to the so-called King's Chamber by way of the left-hand stairs up through the corbelled gallery.

For argument's sake, we will call this room the Chamber of Set. There is nothing inside this great space, but for a large sarcophagus of red granite; the orientation of its longest sides is south to north. The walls and floor are of black granite. Priests would be present to aid Pharaoh as he was placed in the sarcophagus, head to the south and feet to the north, which signifies the position of the pole star in the north.

After the chanting of prayers, the Sem Priest would then signal the commencement of the ritualistic ordeal Pharaoh would be put through. Four priests would position themselves at each corner of the sarcophagus, and, placing their fingertips on the edge of the coffer, they would intone specific vowel sounds. According to John Reid, a specialist in the study of sonics, "When certain sounds are played in close proximity to granite, these sound frequencies excite the crystals within the stone, which makes them resonate."

Given that the entire chamber and sarcophagus is of granite, this would have brought about a physical, mental, and spiritual change within the body and mind of the king. His very being would be saturated with sound. His limbs and vessels would be tingling because of the vibrations of this deliberate orchestration of tones, each priest emitting a prescriptive dose.

At a particular point, the Sem Priest would indicate to the wahabs to gently remove Pharaoh from the coffer, and in a backwards or reversed mode, the king would leave the Chamber of Set. He would be fully prepared for his next phase of rebirth and renewal, which would take place in the room below, which we will call the Chamber of Horus.

Walking backwards down the right-hand side of the corbelled gallery, reversing along a corridor between the double stairway, bending double and still in reverse, Pharaoh would enter this next chamber. He would not see the priesthood, but would be aware of yet more chanting and intoning of carefully chosen notes which once again resonate through the granite. The walls of this chamber are lined with pale grey granite and in the centre of the floor is placed a gleaming white limestone sarcophagus of similar proportions to that of the coffer in the Chamber of Set.

Once again Pharaoh is guided and placed in the coffer. His emotions run high as he is plunged into the great abyss of the celestial waters. In trance, his body sleeps, but his soul is awake. It is active on its own plane; the body is in the background of a different matter. This mind-altering state has rid him of his fragile body, as he is absorbed into the realms of nonbeing. He is awakened to the superconsciousness of that which IS, and everything that is portrayed is of the events of the inner world by way of a mirroring. His conditions of focus are being determined by these emotional states.

He has been subjected to the very force of the Primum Mobile, and with this seventh ray of consciousness he has received complete initiation into the "living death." Thus, he has achieved the freedom of the spirit brought through to the plane of matter. He is free, empowered, and stands taller and greater amongst his fellow man.

In those days, a Pharaoh was a man alone. He would have had the counsel of his Sem and the input of the vizier, etc., but after a Heb Sed festival of rebirth and renewal, this would make him suprahuman.

The very design of the Great Pyramid sets a platform for a magnificent and mind-altering stage for a special event. One can only enter this great monument today, to realise that there is something very special and poignant about the peculiar design quality of these tunnels and shafts, all hidden from public view. Who else but the ancient Egyptians would fashion a tunnel on the god Set's constellation of Ursa Major?

As we enter this great mound of calculated pieces of stone, our bodies twist and double; we crawl and walk tall as did the pharaohs of old. We reach the inner sanctum, totally exhausted, and stand over an empty granite box where the king would have been plunged into his own kind of oblivion. We too are laid waste in this empty room, and some of us wonder what it's all about. Then, as we make our way down again to the outside world, we find that, secretly and subliminally, the pyramid has given us back something else, in return for the energy we gave it, to breathe new life into the Great Tunnels of Set.

Path to Set and Horus
Journey to the Tunnels of Set

Don your white robe and tie yellow, black, and red cords around your waist. This will be in respect of the Neters you will be working with.

Build your pylons and make the sign of the ankh in the air above your head. On the lintel of the portal, hieroglyphs of Horus and Set appear:

Commit them to memory. This symbol is charged; look at each mark and take it within. As you utter your secret name, your journey takes you to the House of Eternity where you will commune with the gods Horus and Set. This is a gateway that will take you to the heart of your initiatory realm. You will learn how to focus on their energy as you are drawn in.

You arrive, and stand in the brilliant sunshine under a sky of blinding cobalt blue. Djehuty greets you, jubilantly explaining that Pharaoh is to undergo a sacred ritual, and together you make your way to the Rostau Valley where many nobles and their ladies have gathered, all dressed in their finest garments, eagerly waiting for Pharaoh's entrance.

Drums beat out a rolling rhythm; fanfares of trumpets hail the entrance of many members of priesthoods holding small statuettes of their respective Neters, all in preparation for their king's arrival. The air is thick with the smell of kyphi incense.

Then you see a face you recognize; it is Khaemwaset. He is robed in full regalia; his crisp white tunic rustles freely in the soft breeze. His gold belt of aurechalcum glints in the sun. Hanging over his broad brown shoulders is the pelt of a leopard, signifying that he is the Sem Priest.

Pharaoh steps down from a litter carried by four Nubians. His body servant is at hand to adjust the jewelled pectoral suspended around his royal neck; he then realigns the pleats of the king's gold-encrusted kilt that makes little clinking sounds at his every movement. In his right hand he holds a golden flail and in his left, the crook.

Pharaoh is regal from the Sekhemti, white and red crown of Heru-Sutekh, symbols of Upper and Lower Khemit, right down to the woven golden sandals on his feet. His body has been oiled with precious fragrance that wafts around him like an invisible cloud.

The air is stilled the moment Pharaoh takes his first step forward, his golden sandaled feet softly touching Khemit's dry sand. The crowds look on with jubilation as the king processes onward, the last rays of Ra shining upon this god-man.

Meanwhile, you are ushered forward by Djehuty and Khaemwaset where you join the royal company, and together with them walk in meditation to the temple on the skyline, the House of Eternity.

You are curious to know why you should be chosen to walk with the king in this sacred ritual. The path is strewn with spices and flowers that give off a heavenly scent as they are crushed underfoot.

The House of Eternity casts a great shadow across the plateau as Ra goes to the west, but nevertheless the heat of the day hangs heavy in the air.

Now priests are all around you, and the continuous chanting and the smell of incense is making you feel dizzy and confused. Khaemwaset stands before you, anointing your forehead, temples, throat, and the back of your neck with the sacred oil of messeh. He utters:

"Uat ap-na au.
The ways I have opened
Ah, ab [utter your secret name]
Hail heart of [utter your secret name]."

You look around you. Gone is the pharaoh, if ever he was there; just Lord Djehuty and Khaemwaset walk the final steps with you, divine is this level. Facing you is the portal of the House of Eternity, above the door is carved the hieroglyph for the Neter Hapy:

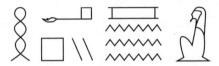

You turn to face Djehuty. From his eyes tears are falling, from his lips he says:

"Seeker, I have been your guide, and Khaemwaset your Sem Priest. You have shown true courage throughout all the paths put your way. We have travelled far together, across the deserts and the wastelands. I have watched you grow from innocence to the wise Seeker. You have matched the many priests, and eclipsed them in their wisdom. It is now time to venture forward where you alone will run the gamut. You alone will know the secrets and celebrate your life's renewal."

Djehuty raises his hand upwards, continuing:

"This was Khufu's greatest temple, not a grave to hold his body, not a place of lasting sadness, but a house to venture inwards. Now, say farewell to *all* your past lives."

You turn to face the portal and walk towards your future ending. Dark is the passage inside and you pause, adjusting your eyes to the dimness, groping your way along a narrow hallway that leads to a ladder.

You climb up five rungs then, stooping forward, bending your body double, you slowly crawl like a wolf. Upwards you go, seeing nothing but darkness, hearing nothing but your pounding heart.

Seventy-one steps you have scrambled, and at last you stand, lifting your gaze up to a cavern gently lit by a suffused amber glow. This cathedral-like chamber is immense, holy, a shrine in itself; it is the grand corbelled gallery. Such are these majestic layers flowing in upon you, they hold peculiar sounds that filter upwards, sounds that come from right below you, causing you to almost swoon with pleasure.

Deep within the bedrock of this temple are giant teeth of stone that act like tuning forks, forever adjusting the monument as the earth moves with the stellar.

Your gaze now drifts to stairways on the sidewalls centred by a deeper hallway. You are perplexed and not sure which way to go. Masked and cloaked in the skin of a leopard stands a Sem Priest, waiting for you; he ushers you towards the left-hand stairway. There are ninety-three steps leading to a wooden ladder with seven rungs. You pause now above the gallery to catch your breath, then push onwards. Stooping once again you make your way through a short tunnel, then stand tall for a brief moment before stooping again along another short tunnel, and eventually enter the huge inner sanctum of Sutekh, child of Nut. The aroma of frankincense and myrrh wafts around you.

In this great room stands assembled a priesthood, poised and alerted to test you to your limits. The walls of the chamber are lined with black granite that is ringing with sound. Centred on the floor is a large red granite coffer, empty, ready. To the sound of a drum, voices ring out in strange intonations as the chanting rises; you are filled with a floating sensation.

Two priests stand on either side of you and gently lift you by your elbows, lowering you into this bed of stone. Your fragile body is carefully positioned. Your head is laid in the south and your feet face the direction north.

In this chasm, you lay suspended while the Sem Priest utters soul sounds. A wahab priest stands at each corner with their hands placed lightly on the edges of the sacred coffer intoning vowel sounds for your rebirth, sounds that penetrate the very core of your being.

No more do you see the priesthood as you experience altered states of consciousness. The chamber is now completely saturated with prime sounds that excite the crystals in the granite, causing the coffer to vibrate. Your body is in momentary suspension; you shudder as the vibration from the coffer penetrates your body. A strange white powder is drifting around you and through the fine dust you see the walls turn transparent!

You are now raised to cosmic levels where much mystery is told to you. You are listening to multiformat through a different time continuum.

Then a voice from within tells you:

"This is only preparation; this is not the final setting."

Two priests are now gently raising you out of the coffer where you stand erect, and in a daze you leave Sutekh's sacred chamber with the Sem Priest and return to the corbelled gallery, and in a manner directed, you walk backwards down the stairway to the narrow-halled entrance for the next phase of your journey, to the reverse side of your soul.

Backwards you walk, bending down double, through a tunnel to the hallowed space of Horus's twin brother, Set. The walls of this chamber are lined with grey granite, and centred in the floor of this chamber is a white and gleaming coffer hewn from pure limestone.

Again a drum sounds and voices ring out in strange intonations that fill you with a floating sensation as the chanting rises. Two priests stand on either side of you, again holding your elbows; they gently lift, then lower you into this bed of stone. Your fragile body is carefully positioned; your head is laid in the south and your feet face the direction north.

No more do you see the priesthood. In this chasm you lay suspended, backwards through a void you plummet, deeper still your body's falling, through the inner space of nothing.

Then, crossing over a deeper chasm, you feel the might of serpent current, and within this realm are the tunnels of Set. To primeval times, mirrored backwards into the void of formless consciousness, you tumble right down into the abyss. You now sense a fearsome crushing that awakens ancient notions, where the polar axis loses all meaning.

Much exalted by this magick, you slip into a dream state, thus awakening the ancient serpent that surrounds the crown of your forehead. You have awakened the powers from nonbeing.

Around you scarlet dust is swirling from a black sun that never sets. Chamber shafts have now turned into tunnels, each emitting a special tuning. The star Sobdet is beckoning to you and you feel your body being pulled up towards her radiance. Blue-tinged rays now flood the chamber, scattering light within your being. You are now becoming the milk of stardust, and from within this you are looking down a spiral structure as your new being crosses the stellar ocean.

Still in sight is the greater temple, glowing like a crystal in the vortex. Another tunnel opens further and you find your form spinning, tumbling, falling through it towards a brilliant red corona.

There, before your eyes, is the Great Bear; Alkaid, Alioth and Miza, Alcor, Phecda follows Megrez, then comes Merak and now Dhube. Wondrous is their star formation suspended in the outer limits.

You are joyous as the stars of Nut look at them, hanging in perfect friendship. Being in this cosmic realm makes you tremble with such passion. The closer you move amongst them, the more mystery is unfolded; you are listening to the words of stardust.

Then a voice is heard, a whisper coming from the starry distance, coming from the empty vastness. You are wrapped in visions, lost in dreaming, and you hear yourself saying:

"I see the broad red stellar pathway, a pathway of the gods and shadows. Now I hear a voice that calls me; I hear his voice boom through the starlight."

Gone are the priests from the chamber of Horus who were with you all the way, and in front stands Djehuty, his hand extended. As you take it, you feel a reawakening, a renewal of your body's life force. He utters:

"Di-ek eni awik kher ka-ek,
Shesepi su ankhi yemef,
I ashek reni er heh,
Ben hehif em rek."

"Give me your hands, holding thy spirit,
That you may receive it and may live by it,
We call now upon thy name,
And it shall never fail."

You leave the House of Eternity the way you entered; moving down through the Tunnels of Set you walk, standing tall for a fleeting moment, then stooping and crawling. You have walked within the shape of the adze, the ritual tool of Set. You have walked the Path of Ursa Major and, in doing so, you have become an instrument of the Neters. But your exit is through the very outstretched paws of the Great Sphinx. You look up at him in amazement! Djehuty is by your side smiling.

Tears fill your eyes and a strange lightness fills your heart. The journey has been long and hard at times, but you faced the challenges and emerged stronger. You stand here now as have other Seekers of the Mysteries, freed from the limitations of your fears, doubts, and ignorance. True insight has been attained, of the Self, and in doing so you have touched the very essence of your beloved Neters. Beloved pilgrim, your place amongst the Imperishable Stars is assured, have no doubt of that. You have proved yourself worthy and pure of heart!

Construct your pylons and walk through the portal to your world of familiar regions. Utter your secret name to the gods and seal the door behind you.

TWENTY

LEGEND OF BASTET

Other temples are greater and more costly,
but none more pleasing to the eye than this.

HERODOTUS, DESCRIPTION OF PER BASTA

Bastet, the cat goddess, was a much-loved deity whose main cult centre was at Bast (the Greek Bubastis) in the northeast Delta. The main temple, Per-Bastet (House of Bastet) gave its name to the town, and in its heyday this cult centre had several temples, including one dedicated to Mihos, a lion god who was supposed to be a child of Bastet. Today it is a heavily ruined complex, but during the time of Herodotus in the fifth century BCE its splendour gave cause for much pleasure. The children of Bastet, the cat in its myriad of forms, were held in high affection by the ancient Egyptians and were accorded similar dignified burial rites as their human counterparts. Several large cat cemeteries have been found at Bast as well as other sites.

Bast was a strategically important place that also gained political prominence during Dynasty 22, as the country's rulers originated from there. In the Late Period, it became the eighteenth nome of Lower Egypt.

During the Pyramid Age, Bastet was strongly connected with kingship and was invoked as royal protectress in the Pyramid Texts to enable the king to reach the sky. In the Coffin Texts of the Middle Kingdom, this role expanded to include royal courtiers.

As an "Eye of Ra," this Neter's protective qualities were well illustrated in various historical texts as the pharaoh took on her aggressive qualities to smite his enemies. For example, Amenhotep II slaughters his enemies "like the victims of Bastet along the road cut by the god Amun."

Bastet's original form may have been of a lioness that changed over time and in the first millennium BCE she transformed into the more benevolent cat. She is usually portrayed as a woman with a cat's head, holding a sistrum, and at times accompanied by kittens at her feet. The name Bastet means "She of Bast" and the hieroglyphic representation of her name is of a sealed alabaster jar, possibly holding perfume oils.

Herodotus gives a colourful and detailed account of the Festival of Bast, where thousands of men and women travelled on boats, riotously enjoying music, singing, clapping, and dancing. When they passed towns, the women would call out rude jokes to the shore-bound and displayed more than a bit of cheek for their delectation. When they reached Bast, they made their sacrifices of various animals, and drank as much wine as they were able to. Sounds rather like an evening's entertainment in some of our modern cities!

Herodotus equated Bastet with the Greek goddess Artemis because of the similarities in their popularity amongst the populous and the exuberance of their festivities, but it is difficult to see where the connection is; not even their sacred animals were similar (i.e., it was the bear for Artemis and the cat for Bastet). Bastet's worship remained unabated throughout Khemit's long history and was carried across the Greco-Roman world by her conquerors. Like Isis she takes on many identities throughout her travels but at her very core remains essentially a Neter, deeply connected to her people and her land, Khemit.

PATH TO BASTET

Journey to Per-Basta

Don your white robe and tie purple and white cords around your waist. This will be in respect of the Neter you will be working with.

Build your pylons and make the sign of the ankh in the air above your head. On the lintel of the portal, hieroglyphs of Bast-et appear:

Commit them to memory. This symbol is charged; look at each mark and take it within. As you utter your secret name, your journey takes you to the sacred temple at Per-Basta where you will commune with the goddess Bastet. This is a gateway that will take you to the heart of her realm. You will learn how to focus on her energy as you are drawn in.

Djehuty is standing by the banks of the Nile. All around are barges of every description floating leisurely down river, filled with men and women. The men play on pipes while the women shake sistra and tambourines. On other barges, young girls dance and sing and clap their hands. Such is the Feast of Bastet and you have been invited to join in.

A gaily painted barge pulls in to where you are standing with your guardian and together you quickly jump aboard. Another barge swings close to yours, full of jolly swaying young men. One calls out to you, handing you a goblet of beer: "Rejoice and drink to the goddess! Hail Bastet!"'

All along the banks, crowds of villagers have gathered, waving and throwing flower petals into the blue-bright waters. The individual singers of folk songs have now merged into one tumultuous chant as they draw ever closer to the town of Per-Basta, where the thousands of revellers will drink wine of the grape and barley beer and feast to the early hours of the morning.

You sigh contentedly; it is just as you imagined, a true spectacle of sound, scent, and visuals. All who worship on this sacred day pulsate with life joyous, life victorious! A wide smile crosses your lips as you look towards your guardian. He reaches over and trails a finger across your cheek; it conveys such love and gentleness, the like of which is echoed within your heart. You are finally home.

Djehuty then turns to give directions to the rowers to take a side canal. Gleaming water floats before you; two great canals fed from the River Nile sweep around the walls of a glorious red granite structure that regally rises high above the now-clear luminous water. Each canal is a hundred feet wide; its banks are lined with trees that cast their welcome shade on the ever-growing heat of a perfect Khemit day.

The barge steadily pulls into a small jetty that is decorated with bunches of flowers. A deep stairway adorned with sculptures leads up to the temple. Two priestesses dressed in white run down eagerly to greet you and place a garland of jasmine flowers around your neck. The perfume is delicate but heady. They take you by your hand and lead you up to the main gateway of the House of Bastet.

You briefly hesitate to gather your thoughts, and then turn to the priestesses who reassure you all is well.

At the top of the steps you pause and look down; you have steadily and effortlessly climbed sixty feet. The town of Basta looks small indeed!

Through the gateway you walk towards a shaded garden, accompanied by your guardian Djehuty and the two priestesses. They leave you to sit beside a fountain gently spilling its water into a pond of lotus lilies. Around you are lavender bushes and roses of all colours; again the perfume is heady. The silence is broken by a woman's voice.

"Do our gardens please you, Seeker of the Mysteries?"

Standing before you is a regal beautiful woman. Her features are unusually feline; large green eyes sparkle. You think to yourself:

"Judging by her noble raiment, she must be of high ranking." Her robe is of deep purple, sacred and imperial dye prized above all others throughout the millennia, a thing of rare beauty born from the pungent and inglorious mollusk. Around her neck is a collar of silver, more prized than gold. Set deep in its centre is a moonstone the size of a small egg; its milky opalescence mesmerizes you. In her arms she holds a small tabby cat with the same beautiful green eyes.

"I am Jemra Hemet-Netjer, high priestess of our lady's temple."

Standing, you instinctively incline your head towards her, saying:

"I pay homage to you, Jemra Hemet-Netjer."

"In the name of Bastet, Great Cat Goddess, and our mother, we bid you welcome."

The high priestess's eyes look at you intensely.

"You have one more path to walk before you are whole. O Seeker of the Mysteries, I invite you to come with me."

As you leave the garden, you feel the soft fur of a cat as it wraps its slinky body around your legs; purring, it wanders off into nearby rose bushes. You follow the high priestess along a pathway towards some low buildings. An open door at the end leads into a small room; the walls are painted white and the air is cool inside this chamber. The only light coming in is from a small window; in front of it is a small table on which rests a statuette of Bastet in her cat-woman aspect. On the windowsill is a purple-coloured vase containing fresh jasmine; the scent of jasmine and lavender that pervades the room has a calming and sensual effect on you. Against a wall is a simple palette, over which is thrown a luscious purple cover. The colour vibrates in the half-light of the room. All the while the high priestess has been standing there observing you. Finally she breaks the silence, saying:

"Moon foods will be brought to you to partake of; these are the white foods that will cleanse and prepare you for your next and final initiatory path, as all the priests and priestesses of the House of Bastet have trod before you."

A priest enters the room holding a wooden platter that is placed carefully on the bed. You look at the strange mix of various cheeses, sublimated curds, almond buns, small dairy biscuits shaped like a crescent moon, and a clay beaker of white liquid. Both high priestess and priest leave you to eat. You search within yourself for any hint of fear or doubt, but none exists. Whatever is to come, you will meet with clarity and willingness, perfect trust, and perfect love. The liquid is first to tempt you, but you find it quite foul-tasting and quickly mask the strange flavour with a crescent-moon biscuit; they are so delicious in taste you wish there were more. Next you try an almond bun, which you dip in the curds; the taste too is strange but palatable. Out of the corner of your eye you notice a bright silvery light enter through the window, which now fills the room. It does not disturb you but serves only to heighten the sense of inner calm—fulfillment.

You then begin to lose all sense of time and drift into a euphoric state; you feel as if your skin is slowly and carefully being pealed from your body, but there is no pain. Your skin is now a deathly pale shade.

There is a gentle knock at the door, which silently opens by itself. Standing there is a blue-cloaked and hooded figure holding a large bowl of tepid water. The figure indicates that you wash yourself thoroughly and replace your white robe with one of fine-mist linen.

In this dreamlike state, you cleanse your body, don your robe, and leave the chamber with this mysterious figure. He seems familiar and you try to take a closer look, but the mysterious figure backs away from you.

Outside, the full moon of Djehuty sends his beams to surround you. You are now aware of other cloaked figures behind you and, together with them, you proceed through the vastness of the temple, across a great expanse of courtyard to the southwest place of worship, and you make your way to Bastet's inner sanctum.

The portals of the goddess swing open; the entire priesthood has gathered to witness these rites. All eyes are on you.

You cross hallways to the vestry and as you walk, wispy tendrils of smoke slowly swirl around your feet. You walk onwards and upwards towards a violet vapour. Again the scent of fresh jasmine and lavender fills the air around you. Then, like a silver thread through darkness, your astral Sa leaves your body and travels to far-off places. Your mortal body is cloaked in outer shadows; whispering phantoms from these shadows ask you:

"Why do you enter this sanctum?"

You make to answer using your secret name, replying:

"I am (utter your secret name), seeking the mystery of past ages."

From the shadows tall and regal, the high priest followed by the high priestess walk towards you. With these words he utters to you:

"I will be your guide from now hence, protecting all your inner levels. I will teach you ancient bylaws of the sacred Mystery Schools."

The high priest takes your hand as you cross the threshold to the inner shrine to Bastet. In front of you is a colossal silver statue of the cat goddess herself in her female form. In her left hand she holds the aegis and in her right hand a sistrum that is tinkling softly. Around her feet are jasmine oil-filled lamps that cense and illuminate her beautiful form.

Power pulses through your body, and light turns into velvety darkness, awakening the mystery in the core of your being. Your heartbeat echoes that of the temple's—resonant and rich in its rhythm. The high priest urges you to take steps forward, and you walk anti-sunrise sevenfold around the goddess's giant form. The black and white tiles mesmerise you with every step you take. You ask yourself how many others have sought to receive initiation on this path of the higher mental plane. The doors open on the inner planes, waiting for you to pass through them. What is it to be?

You now pause, taking deep breaths, whilst the high priest says:

"I will be your guide through your final rebirth."

Through a hallowed secret portal between the silver feet of Bastet you walk in a trancelike state. Leading you downward into darkness, you tread the many steps of trial. A feeling of melancholy washes over you as once again you are being stripped of the many veneers of a lifetime of habits, ill feelings towards others, and distrust of your fellow beings. You watch as your outer shell dissolves. Echoed in your illumined back brain is the divine spark loosening your psyche, awakening your ancient pineal gland; only through darkness can your dormant sleeping brain be reawakened to the secret rites of mystery.

You now drift in a vacuum, and around you swirls a different ether. Once unborn to live and flourish from the spaces wrapped in shadows, in true darkness you are now cleansed by Bastet.

Where so many priests have perished, you emerge victorious. You let out a long deep breath of relief and satisfaction. Life fills your lungs as you are birthed into being. Your eyes open as you utter a cry of wonder. The world appears as if it has been washed clean in the sacred waters of Nun. Each element sparkles with the intensity of a flawless jewel; colours throb with a vibrancy and sensuality. You just drink it all in, savouring the experience like a refreshing drink after an eternity in the desert wastes. Truly it feels like a rebirth into a new life. You close your eyes once more to give silent thanks to Bastet. Your reveries are broken as emissaries of the goddess gather around you for the final ritual.

The high priest and priestess are present as a priest anoints your forehead with the oil of messeh. You don a lustrous silk robe of royal purple; on your head is placed a silver circlet made in the form of finely twisted jasmine flowers. On your right wrist is placed a silver bracelet in the form of a recumbent cat. Around your neck is hung an amethyst of deepest purple.

You now stand tall amongst the priesthood of Bastet and, gazing up at the silver form of the goddess, you utter:

"Bast nefer dy ankh
Hail Bast, in visible form,
Casting light into darkness
Sesept em kekui,
I have come before you
i kua ser-ten, uat sesh-tha, ta em hetep.
The path is opened, the earth is at peace.
You are so alive within me."

As she breathes out upon you, the goddess gives her breath of stardust. It sinks deep within you, seeping into every cell and atom. Stars and galaxies explode behind your eyelids; you feel their beginning, and their end. Yet nothing truly dies but only changes form and shape.

You stand there amongst your fellow priests. Cymbals crash and sistra jingle, and voices chant out:

"May you always live with Bastet; may she live within you always!"

Now the musicians play in concert, celebrating your glorious beginning. Passing now through hall and vestry, you walk tall and proud, and emerge into the sunlight of another Khemit day.

Your guardian and friend Djehuty is waiting outside the temple and salutes you. His eyes smile and twinkle with bright amber lights. It is time to leave this wondrous land of sunshine and shadows.

Before you visualise your pylons to walk through the portal to your world of familiar regions, you look back upon the great River Nile. At last you understand what it is to enter into the great and eternal river of existence as it flows towards the infinite horizons. What awaits at journey's end is a beautiful mystery which only your heart can give voice to, and then only in soft whispers. Truly has this ancient land captured your soul in its deep embrace!

Now utter your secret name to the gods and seal the door behind you.

BIBLIOGRAPHY

Ancient Egypt Magazine. "Cult and Funerary Temples," July–August 2000 (issue 2).

———. "The Temple of Horus at Edfu," September–October 2000 (issue 3).

Armour, Robert A. *Gods and Myths of Ancient Egypt.* Cairo: American University in Cairo Press, 1986.

Ashcroft-Nowicki, Dolores. *The Shining Paths.* London: Aquarian/Thorsons, 1983.

Baines J., and J. Malek. *Atlas of Ancient Egypt.* Oxford: Phaidon Press, 1996.

Brunton, Dr. Paul. *A Search in Secret Egypt.* York Beach, Maine: Samuel Weiser, Inc., 1988.

Budge, E A Wallis. *The Book of Opening the Mouth.* London: Trench, Trubner, 1909.

———. *Gods of the Egyptians (Studies in Egyptian Mythology).* London: Dover Publications, 1969.

Draco, Mélusine. *Liber Aegyptius.* London: Ignotus Press, 1998.

Farrell, Nick. *Magickal Pathworking, A Technique of Active Imagination.* St. Paul, Minnesota: Llewellyn Publications, 2004.

Fortune, Dion. *Moon Magick.* London: Aquarian Press, 1956.

Grant, Kenneth. *Cults of the Shadow.* London: Skoob Publishing, 1994.

Griffis-Greenberg, Katherine. *The Guiding Feminine: Goddesses in Ancient Egypt.* London: British Journal, January 1998.

Gurdjieff, G. I. *Meetings with Remarkable Men.* London: Arkana, 1985.

Hart, George. *Dictionary of Egyptian Gods and Goddesses*. London: Routledge, 1986.

Hichens, Robert. *Spell of Egypt*. New York: The Century Co., 1911.

Hope, Murry. *Practical Egyptian Magick*. New York: St. Martin's Press, 1986.

Hornung, Erik. *Conceptions of God in Ancient Egypt: The One and the Many*. Ithaca, New York: Cornell University Press, 1971.

Lawlor, Robert. *Sacred Geometry*. London: Thames & Hudson, 1982.

Morenz, Siegfried. *Egyptian Religion*. Ithaca, New York: Cornell University Press, 1973.

Murray, Margaret. *The Bundle of Life from Ancient Egypt*. London: Sidgwick & Jackson, 1972.

Page, Judith. *The Song of Set*. London: Aeon Publishing, 2000.

———. *The Song of Meri Khem*. Oxford: Mandrake of Oxford, 2007.

———. *The Song of Bast*. (To be published).

Poe, Michael. "Ancient Egyptian Metaphysics" (personal paper).

Redford, Donald B. The *Ancient Gods Speak*: *A Guide to Egyptian Religion*. Oxford: Oxford University Press, 2002.

Rice, Michael. *Egypt's Making: The Origins of Ancient Egypt 5000–2000 BC*, 2nd ed. London: Routledge, 2003.

Richardson, Alan, and B. Walker-John. *The Inner Guide to Egypt*. Woodbury, Minnesota: Llewellyn Publications, 2010. (First published in the United Kingdom in 1991, by Arcania Press.)

Shaw, Ian, and Paul Nicholson. *The British Museum Dictionary of Ancient Egypt*. London: The British Museum, 2002.

Smith, Wilbur. *River God*. Oxford: Pan Books, 1993.

St. George, Elizabeth. *Journey to the Cat Star*. London: Spook Publication, 1990.

Vernus, Pascal. *The Gods of Ancient Egypt*. New York: George Braziller, 1998.

Watterson, Barbara. *The House of Horus at Edfu: Ritual in an Ancient Egyptian Temple*. Stroud, UK: Tempus Publishing, 1998.

———. "Myth and Ritual in the Temple of Horus at Edfu." *Ancient Egypt Magazine*, November–December 2000 (issue 4).

Wilkinson, Richard H. The *Complete Gods and Goddesses of Ancient Egypt*. London: Thames & Hudson, 2003.

Wilkinson, Toby. *Early Dynastic Egypt*. London: Routledge, 2001.

GLOSSARY

Abju: Ancient Egyptian name for *Abydos.*

Abydos: Greek form of *Abju.*

Abyss: The great gulf or void that constitutes the separation of individual consciousness from its universal source. To Cross the Abyss, or transcend the world of subject and object, is to resolve the antinomies of mundane consciousness.

Adze: Ancient ritual object made from iron tektites; it was fashioned in the shape of the constellation *Ursa Major, the Great Bear,* or *the Plough.* This also symbolised the god Set.

Akhet: Season of the inundation in the ancient Egyptian calendar, heralded by the rising of Sirius, the dog-star called Sobdet.

Alcor: Star in the constellation of *Ursa Major.*

Alkaid: Star in the constellation of *Ursa Major.*

Amente: A mythological domain of the dead on the western shore of the Nile.

Amen-em-het: Twelfth Dynastic Pharaohs.

Amun: Ancient local god of Thebes whose name means "the Hidden One," or "the Great Cackler."

Amunhotep I: Founding builder of Luxor Temple.

Andjeti: God in anthropomorphic form originally worshipped in the mid-Delta in the Lower Egyptian nome. Egyptian underworld god. His worship originated in the ninth nome of Lower Egypt. His cult center was at Busiris. Andjety was responsible for the rebirth of the individual in the afterlife. Depicted in anthropomorphic form, he wore a high conical crown sur-mounted by two feather plumes, and bore the crook and flail. Osiris was associated with Andjeti, whose symbols were also the crook and flail as well as the atef crown.

Ankh (or *crux ansata*): The symbol of eternal life in ancient Egypt.

Antef: Early feudal warlord who later became one of the early Pharaohs of Egypt.

Anubis: Greek form of Anpu—dog god deity of the dead.

Apep: See *Apophis.*

Apis: The sacred bull, a theophany of the Ptah-Sokar cult at Mem-phis.

Apophis: A giant mythical serpent with mystical powers who was the enemy of the sun god Ra.

Asar: Ancient Egyptian for *Osiris.* There are over one hundred names of gods that start with the prefix "Asar."

Athyr: Third month of the season of *Akhet,* winter inundation.

Atum: Sun god and creator of the universe. The name Atum car-ries the idea of "totality" in the sense of an ultimate and unal-terable state of perfection.

Aurichalcum: Mysterious red-flecked gold, thought to have origi-nated from the mythical Atlantis.

Auset: Ancient Egyptian name for *Isis*, means "Exceeding Queen or Spirit."

Bakhet: God of the east and summit of the two horizons.

Behdet: Ancient Egyptian for *Edfu.*

Benenet: Ancient mound of earth that sprang out of the first wa-ters.

Chaos: The primal substance that is, paradoxically, by no means substantial, out of which the illusion of formless primordial matter appears to rise.

Chemmis (or Khemmis): Island in the Delta area where Isis gave birth to Horus.

Crook: Emblem of sovereignty and divinity.

Deshert: Red crown of Lower Egypt in the North.

Djed: The ancient Egyptian symbol for stability.

Djedu: Ancient town in the Delta, and nome region of the ancient god, Andjety.

Djinns: Spirit form lower than angels.

Dhube: Star in the constellation of *Ursa Major.*

Edfu: Greek form. Called *Behdet* by the ancient Egyptians, meaning "Exhaltation of Horus."

Enki: (or Ea): "Lord of the Earth," god of Mesopotamia.

Eridu: Cult centre of the Enki triad, located at the head of the present Persian Gulf.

Esna: Cult centre for god Khnemu and goddess Nebtu'u.

Eye of Ra: Term describing the eye of the sun god, which was thought to exist as an independent entity; this symbol was also asscociated with a number of goddesses.

Fayoum: Modern name of Ta-she and Sher-resy.

Flail: Emblem of sovereignty and dignity.

Geb: Earth god and president of the divine tribunal on the kingship according to the Osirian mythology.

Giza: A plateau south of modern Cairo. See *Rostau.*

Great Bear: Another name for *Ursa Major.*

Great Eternal: The unmanifest made pure existence.

Hadit: Chaldean form of Set.

Hapy: God of the annual Nile inundation. The god is shown in human form with aquatic plants on his head.

Haroerus (or Harwer): Also called Heru-ur, translates to "Horus the Elder" in the the Osirian pantheon group.

Hathor: Important cow goddess, whose worship may have originated in predynastic times. Name means "Mansion of Horus"or "House of Horus." She was variously worshipped as a woman with the ears of a cow, as a cow, and as a woman wearing a headdress composed of a wig, horns, and sun disk. Considered the divine mother of each Pharaoh. Main cult centre was based in Denderah.

Heb Sed: An elaborate ceremony of the king's Coronation: his *Sed* festival, or jubilee and ultimate burial, were twice repeated with the different insignia, architecture, and customs of Upper and Lower Egypt. The ceremony of the "Running of Apis" appears to have been closely associated with the Sed festival, but it seems more likely to have been originally a celebration of the festival called the "Birth of the god Sed." The entire nation was deeply concerned with the celebration of these important rites. The festival usually took place thirty years after the king's accession to the throne. However, according to the evidence of the Palermo Stone, the Sed festival was celebrated by some of the archaic kings repeatedly, and at much shorter intervals than the accepted thirty-year period. In order to celebrate this important festival, a special building was erected, called a Sed pavilion. This included a throne room and a robing room in which the king changed his garments and insignia according to the various double rites connected with the two lands. But most important was the *Heb Sed* court, flanked on both sides with the chapels of the Upper and Lower Egyptian gods of each nome. The king would run in the open space between the two rows of shrines, dressed alternatively in the insignia colours of white for Upper, and red for Lower Egypt. This ritual race around the "field" was repeated four times as the ruler of the south, and four times as ruler of the north. It is suggested that the "field" represented Egypt and the ritual race perhaps signified to all those present his claim as possessor of the land.

To this was added the further impetus for national fertility; his actions made the land fruitful and productive.

Hedjet: White crown of Upper Egypt in the South.

Heliopolitan Doctrine: Creation myth involving the *Great Ennead* at Iunu (Heliopolis). The creator god Atum emerges from the primeval waters of Nun, engenders himself, and subsequently undertakes the creation of the first life through various means—such as masturbating, spitting, or sneezing. The first of the nine gods to emerge are the personification of air (Shu) and water/moisture (Tefnut). They in turn give birth to Nut and Geb, whose progeny consists of Osiris, Set, Isis, and Nephthys.

Hem-Neter: A title given to one who serves all the Neters.

Henu boat: A magickal boat that was never meant to sail on water, but was driven by light.

Hermopolitan Doctrine: Creation myth involving four pairs of primeval snake and frog deities (the Ogdoad of Khemenu) who emerged from the eternal chaos, and were named as Nun and Nunet, Heh and Hehet, Kek and Keket, and Amun and Amunet. These eight primeval gods were considered divine ancestors who were believed to be buried under Medinet Habu, and honoured with libations every decade by the later pharaohs. Tahuti had his main cult centre at Khemenu.

Heru-Khuti: Ancient Egyptian god of the east.

Heru-Sutekh: Twin form of *Horus* and *Set*.

Heru: Ancient Egyptian for *Horus*.

Hetch: Light or brilliance coming from *Nekheb*.

Het-Hert: Ancient Egyptian for *Hathor*.

Hidden One: A reference given to *Amun*; his form cannot be known.

Horus: Greek form of *Heru*.

House of Eternity: Great Pyramid of Khufu.

Hypostyle Hall: This was a large temple court filled with columns. It was entered via the pylons into the open courtyard and then into the Hypostyle Hall. The Hypostyle was symbolic of the primeval swamp at the edge of the Mound, the columns representing papyrus plants, present either as open papyrus flowers or closed papyrus buds. The temple itself was a physical expression of the act of creation, and its architecture reflected the sacred plan in three dimensions. The use of light and spatial dimensions gave the impression of passing through the sacred landscape until the Holy of Holies was reached, the Inner Sanctuary.

Imhotep: Vizier of Netjerikhet (Djoser) and architect of the step pyramid. An individual greatly respected for his wisdom and knowledge, eventually becoming deified after his death. The god Imhotep was considered to have influence over wisdom, writing, and medicine, and for that reason was linked with Tahuti and Ptah. The Greeks identified him with Asclepius. His cult centres were based at Saqqara, Karnak, and Deir El-Bahri.

Imy-ut (or *imiut*): Ancient fetish associated with the god Anpu, consisted of a stuffed, headless skin of an animal (usually a feline) tied to a pole mounted in a pot. Earliest mentions of the fetish occur during the First Dynasty (3100-2890 BCE).

Ineb-hedj: An ancient limestone wall built by Aha. Also known as *Menes.*

Ir-Nkhn: Ancient Egyptian for *Nekhen.*

Iry-Pat: Sacred kings who originated from Sumer.

Isa: Ancient form of *Isis.*

Isis: Greek form of *Isa.*

Isit-Nefert: Second wife of Rameses II, and mother of *Khaemwaset.*

Ka: Ancient Egyptian term for a spiritual essence.

Karnak: Ancient name, Nesut-Towi, "Throne of The Two Lands," and site of the temple to the god Amun.

Kagemni: Was, according to his *Instruction,* vizier of the Fourth Dynasty Pharaoh Snofru (2613–2589 BCE), father of Khufu.

Khaemwaset: Favourite son of Ramesses II and High priest of Ptah in *Men-nefer.*

Khem: A name applied to Egypt as the black or red land. The black or red Nilotic mud that literally formed Egypt.

Khemit: See *Khem.*

Khentamenthes: Ancient dog god, and other form of Set in Abydos.

Khepresh: Great war crown.

Kher-heb: Priest, and lector and master of mortuary rituals.

K-hert: Sacred Book of the Dead.

Khoiak: Fourth month in the season of *Akhet.*

Khonsu: His original name means "navigator," associated with the moon and healing.

Khufu: Reigned between 2551–2528 BCE, Old Kingdom. He was the pharaoh who built the Great Pyramid.

Kom el-Ahmar: Modern name for *Nekhem.*

Labyrinth: A complicated irregular structure with many passages all designed to create confusion.

Luxor: Modern Arabic name for Thebes.

Ma'at: Goddess personifying truth, justice, and cosmic harmony. Representations of Ma'at show her in the guise of a woman wearing an ostrich feather in her hair, an upright feather, or the plinth she sat upon (representing the Primeval Mound). The pharaohs ruled through her authority and the vizier held the title of "Priest of Ma'at."

Mamissi (Coptic: "birth place," "birth house"): Building attached to certain temples, examples being at Edfu, Denderah, and Philae. These buildings (the Ptolemaic ones at least) were composed of a small temple surrounded by a colonnade with screes in between the columns, where rituals were performed connected with the marriage of the goddess or birth of the child god.

Mammon: Regarded as the god of wealth and influence.

Manu: God of the west and summit of the two horizons.

Mastaba: Term given to the step pyramid of Zoser.

Medinet Habu: Ancient Djamet. Temple complex dating from the New Kingdom to the Late Period (1550–332 BCE). Situated at the southern end of the Theban west bank, opposite modern Luxor. The earliest part of the temple complex was a small temple built by Hatsepshut (1473–1458 BCE) and Thutmose III (1479–1425 BCE).

Medula Oblongata: A bundle of nerves in the brain in a formation known as the "decussation of the pyramids."

Megrez: Star in the constellation of *Ursa Major.*

Memphite Doctrine: Creation doctrine thought to originate early in Egyptian history, but the version available to us is eighth century BCE. It was inscribed on a basalt slab used as a millstone, later given the appellation "Shabaka Stone," after the Twenty-Fifth Dynasty Pharaoh Shabaka who commissioned it. Ptah, the supreme being in this version, brings creation into being through thought and utterance (heart and mind). It deviated from other creation doctrines in being a highly spiritual concept.

Menes: Also known as Aha.

Men-nefer: Ancient Egyptian form of *Memphis.*

Mentuhotep: Eleventh Dynasty kings.

Merak: Star in the constellation of *Ursa Major.*

Meretseger: Theban cobra goddess, whose name means "She Who Loves Silence." Her main cult centre was on the mountain (called "the Lady of the Peak") overlooking the Valley of the Kings and included the whole of the Theban necropolis. Her worship was most popular amongst the workmen of Deir el-Medina.

Meshenti: Regal crown of Set.

Mer-wer: Lake at Fayoum.

Mesca: Skin of a bull.

Messeh: Sacred oil of the crocodile used for anointing of kings and queens even to this day.

Mesxet: Star in the constellation of *Ursa Major.*

Metchem: Sacred eye unguent used in the Opening of Mouth Ceremony.

Mut: Goddess and consort of *Amun.*

Mystery Play: Sacred play of Osiris performed in Abydos in the ancient month of Khoaik.

Naqada: North of Thebes, ancient cult center of Set.

Narmer: One of the last predynastic kings associated with the unification of Upper and Lower Egypt.

Natron (ancient name, *net-jeryt,* "belonging to god"): Used mainly for embalming and purification. It is a naturally occurring sodium carbonate/sodium chloride found at the Wadi Natrun, north of modern-day Cairo.

Nebt-Hut: Egyptian form of *Nephthys.*

Nefertum: God of the primeval lotus blossom and son to Ptah and Sekhmet in the triad of Memphis.

Nekheh: Ra.

Nekhbet: Vulture goddess of Nekheb, upholding the king's sway in Upper Egypt.

Nekhen: Now modern Kom el-Ahmar.

Nemes: Band or fillet, symbol of the "light of Nekheb."

Nephthi (or *Nephthys* in Greek): Fifth child of Nut and Geb, according to the Osirian pantheon mythology.

Nephthys: Greek form of Nebt-Hut.

Nesut-Towi: See *Karnak.*

Neter: The ancient Egyptian word that we would equate with god or goddess. But Neter's exact translation is "Abstract Principle" or "Divine Principle" and is not a male or female word.

Nilometric Cubit: Ancient measures that are featured in the Luxor Temple as black stones symbolizing Set.

Nomes: Pharaonic Egypt was divided into forty-two administrative districts, or nomes. Each nome had principal deities. In ancient Egyptian, sepats.

Nu (or *Nun*): God personifying the primeval waters out of which emerged the creator god. Nu is the "father to all gods," but this emphasises only his unrivalled antiquity as an element of the Egyptian cosmos. In terms of importance, he is superseded by the creator sun god *Atum.*

Nun: A being of ancient Egypt, believed to symbolize the primeval watery abyss.

Nu'it: "Infinite Space and the Infinite Stars thereof." In a metaphysical sense, Nu'it is the continuum of paradise that results from the resolution of mundane being into the elements of non-being. Nu'it is represented as a human female form arched over the earth as in the Stele of Revealing. In a more specialised and magickal sense, she is the complement of Set. She is north, and compares with Set, whose opposite is Horus in the south.

Nut: See *Nu'it.*

Ombos: The Set-worshipping tribes occupying a large area in Upper Egypt called Ombos. This area was also famous for the mining of gold.

Opening of Mouth Ceremony: A long and complex rite in which links were established or renewed with the soul of the departed king. It also has very strong Setian implications.

Opet: Patron goddess of eastern Thebes. Also the name given to the Opet Temple in Karnak.

Ophidian: A member of the serpentine order of reptiles.

Osirian: A follower of Osiris.

Osiris: Greek form of *Asar* and *Wasir.*

Osireion: A mysterious subterranean building situated behind the Great Temple of Sety I.

Pathworking: Astral journey undertaken to gain insight or knowledge. The scene is set before the journey begins via a visualisation.

Peribsen: A king of the Second Dynasty.

Peristyle: Term used to describe a type of open court surrounded by an internal colonnade.

Pesh-en-Kef: Associated with Set's forked tail. Usually made from a salmon-pinkish stone called carnelian, and commonly used in *Opening of Mouth Ceremony.*

Pharaoh: Derived from Har-Iu, which means "the Coming Son of a two-fold nature," and of the two IU Houses.

Phecda: Also known as Phad, star in the constellation of Ursa Major.

Pineal gland: Cosmic eye.

Proyet: A season of sowing—springtime.

Ptah: God of Memphis and part of the triad of Nerfertum and Sekhmet.

Ptah-Sokar: Another name for Ptah, associated with mortuary statues.

Ptolemaic: Greco-Egyptians.

Quema: Sacred incense to Set from Nekhen.

Ra: See *Re*.

Rameses II: Third king of the Nineteenth Dynasty and greatest of all the nonroyal-blood kings of ancient Egypt. He was part of a long succession of Setian followers.

Re: Creator sun god of Khenemu (or Heliopolis).

Re-Heru-Khuti: God of the noonday sun.

Rostau: Necropolis containing the pyramid fields; was known as the Duat. A gateway, or entrance.

Royal placenta bundle: The king's placenta, called the "Sacred Bundle of Life," is taken and preserved at the time of his birth. It is kept, wrapped in the form of a kidney shape, for the entirety of the king's life. Ceremonially carried on a high pole by the *Sem Priest* at all festive occasions, it is buried with the king at the point of his death.

Sacred Book of Per-t em hru: commonly known as the Book of the Dead.

Sacred Bundle: See *Royal placenta bundle*.

Sahu: Ancient Egyptian name for Orion.

Salamander: Elemental spirit living within fire.

Saqara: A plateau overlooking the ancient city of Men-nefer. Its vast courtyard or "field" was used for the celebration of the *Heb Sed* festival.

Seb-Hur: Instrument of Anubis, used in Opening of Mouth Ceremony. It symbolized Horus, the Great Star, and god of the south.

Sekhmet: Lion-headed goddess, consort to Ptah and mother to Nerfertum. Part of the triad of Memphis. She is also associated with healing of the bones and with battle.

Sekhmet-Montu: War god of Thebes and linked with

Sekhemti: The red and white crowns of Upper and Lower Egypt produced the Double Crown, a combination of the two emblems.

Sem Priest: The chief or high priest. He also held the first and most honourable station as the one who offered sacrifice and libation in the temple, the highest post. He appears to have been called "the prophet" and his title in the hieroglyphic legends is "Sem." The Sem Priest was the only person who was lawfully allowed to kill the king if he proved unable to continue to rule the land of Khem. This would be a result of not being able to meet the test of the Heb Sed, becoming gravely ill, or perhaps being mortally wounded in battle. The most famous Sem Priest was Setne Khaemwaset, favourite and most royal son of Rameses II. Apart from having the responsibility for arranging the many Heb Sed festivals for his father, the king, this particular priest was probably the first Egyptologist of those times to actually set about restoring the Saqara plateau. This would have included the many pyramids and temples, some of which were already two thousand years old.

Serapeum: See *Usir-Hapuy.*

Set (or Sut): The primordial god of the ancient Egyptians; no earlier god exists in the recorded history of the present human race. The word "soot" is derived from this incalculably ancient name. Set is also the prototype of Shaitan or Satan, god of the south, whose star is Sothis. Set, or Sut (literally meaning "black") is the chief colour (or kala) of Set. Black indicates the dark mysteries of this god, which were originally enacted in the underworld, "netherworld," or Amonta. The god is Lord of Amonta, or "hidden land"—in other words, hell. Hell is the epitome of subconsciousness, and therefore, of the True Will or Hidden Sun, the sun behind the sun symbolised by the Star of Set, Sothis (see also *Shaitan*).

Setian: A follower or worshipper of the god Set.

Setereion: Authors' re-naming of Osireion.

Sety I: Second king of the Nineteenth Dynasty, and father to Rameses II.

Shaitan: The god of the Yezidi, who personified the star Sothis or Sobdet. The rising of this star heralded the inundation of the River Nile, which brought blessed relief to a sun-stricken land.

Shaman: An early priest who would adopt the guise of an animal by wearing its skin, horns, and tail. The carrying of totem animals later developed into the standards bearing the emblems of the popular deities of the regions, or nomes.

Shemu: Harvest season.

Sher-resy: Ancient name for *Fayoum*.

Shu: God of sunlight and air. Shu takes a human form wearing a plume (which is also the hieroglyph for his name) on his head, and with his arms raised, supporting the sky goddess Nut, whom he holds apart from her consort, the earth god Geb.

Sirius: A star in the constellation of Canis Major, and is one of the brightest stars in our night sky. Being only eight-and-a-half light years from the Earth also means it is one of our nearest neighbours.

Sistrum (Seshesht): Musical instrument associated with Hathor, used by women primarily when participating in rituals or ceremonial activities. Two types of sistrum have been found, hooped and naos shaped with the head commonly found on the handle. Plural: sistra.

Smayu Net Set: Ancient name for the "Companions of Set."

Sobek: Crocodile god whose cult centre was Fayoum. He was also the patron deity of many of the kings of the Thirteenth Dynasty.

Sokar (or Sokaris): Hawk god of the Memphite necropolis, also known as "Lord of the Mysterious Region."

Sothis: See *Sirius*.

Sphinx: Form of a recumbent lion with the head of a royal personage.

Sut: Means "the Opener" and Horus who "shuts" or "closes." Sut is the brother of the sun, Horus.

Sut-Har: Another name for *Set*.

Sutekh: Another name for *Set*.

Sut-Typhon: The taunt flung at the Sut-Typhonians by the Osirians was "orphan," intending to brand them as fatherless in a religious sense because they worshipped only the Mother and Child, who became looked upon as the Harlot and the Bastard. The irony is that it was accepted that the mother of the Christ-child experienced an immaculate conception.

Sylph: Elemental spirit living in air.

Talisman: A charm or amulet; an object supposedly capable of working magick.

Ta-Wer: Exalted Land.

Tefnut: Primeval goddess personifying moisture. She is the female consort of Shu.

Tekenu: Mysterious figure in a hooded, sack-shaped garment that was always present at Opening of Mouth Ceremonies.

Telluric current: Earth energy.

Temenos: From the Greek verb "to cut." A piece of land cut from common uses and dedicated to a god; a sanctuary.

Temu: Cosmic god.

Temu-Heru-Khuti: God of the setting sun.

Terra Firma: Earth.

Thebes: Greek form of modern-day Luxor.

Tun-tet: Ostrich feather, used in Opening of Mouth Ceremony.

Two Horizons: See *Sut-Har*.

U-atch: Sacred oil used for the nostrils of the dead in the Opening of Mouth Ceremony.

Udi-mu: A king of the First Dynasty. He is always depicted wearing the white crown, Hedjet, and dressed in a closely fitted garment. This apparel was to be copied later when depicting the god Osiris. The reign of Udi-mu pre-dates the introduction of the Osirian mythology and religion, as this king's sacred animal was the baboon, i.e., Thoth or Djehuty, in conjunction with the Apis.

Undine: Female water spirit.

Ur-Egypt: Term given to early predynastic Egypt.

Ur-Hekau: "The Mighty One of Spells." The Great Magick Power represented the thigh or khepsh of the Goddess Nut, in which the star dwells. The term Ur-Hekau connects this light with hekt, or heket, the lunar ophidian (serpent), currently represented by the frog, lizard, hare, ape, hyena, and other lunar symbols of change, or magickal transformation. The ancient Egyptians used a magick wand which they called Ur-Hekau. It was in the form of a ram-headed snake. This was the symbol of the "Living Word" that had its origins in feminine nature. The ram was a symbol of Amun, and also the Age of Aries, the hidden god carried over from the previous aeon when the crocodile was the zoötype of Set, the god born of the thigh of Typhon. The custodian of this magickal wand would be the Sem Priest.

Ursa Major: The constellation of the Thigh which typified the birthplace of Light in the Dark of the Abyss. The goddess of the seven stars of Ursa Major, with Set the dog-star as the annual proclaimer of the goddess, were reflected terrestrially as the sixteen sanctuaries of Osiris—eight in Upper Egypt and eight in Lower Egypt. Nut was typified celestially by this constellation. The seven stars of this complex symbolised Night or Typhon and her offspring, to which at a later time was added her first male child, Set or Sothis. It is interesting to note that the adze is shaped in the form of Ursa Major.

Usir-Hapuy: Ancient Egyptian name for *Serapeum.*

Uwas sceptre: A sceptre made in the likeness of the god Set. This emblem of dignity was carried by the pharaoh during ceremonial and state occasions, regardless of whether the king was a follower of this deity.

Wadjet: The cobra goddess of Buto and the guardian and preserver of royal authority over Lower Egypt.

Wahab: The lowest rank of priests in the temple. Nevertheless, they were necessary for the daily working of the temple. All of the priesthood were very conscious about their diet, and in general, "the priests abstained from most sorts of pulse, mutton, and swine's flesh"; and, in their more solemn purifications, even excluded salt from their meals. They were as strict about their ablutions as about their diet. They bathed twice a day and twice during the night, and some were so strict, they would only wash themselves with water which had been tasted by the ibis. Every third day, they would shave their head and entire body. They spared no pains when it came to the promotion of cleanliness. Grand ceremonies of purification took place in preparation for their fasts, many of which lasted from seven to forty-two days. Some would fast for an even longer period. During this time they abstained entirely from meat, herbs, and vegetables. All other extra indulgences were put aside. However, the priests enjoyed great privileges. They paid no taxes, no part of their income was used for the necessary expenses of life, any land they owned was free from all duties, and a state allowance of corn was given to them, as well as provisions from the public stores.

Wasir: Ancient Egyptian form of *Osiris*.

Wep-wa-wet: "Opener of ways" appears originally to have been a war god who led the king to battle, but in later times he became a god of the dead, and was eventually assimilated to Anubis. He is depicted as a wolf standing on a nome standard. He is also the original and chief deity of Abju, a realm later to be usurped by Osiris.

Zep Tepi: A mysterious form of the "First Ones" in ancient Egypt.

Zoser: The second king of the Third Dynasty, circa 2630–2611 BCE, son of Kha-Sekhemwy, a Setian king.

TO WRITE TO THE AUTHORS

If you wish to contact the author or would like more information about this book, please write to the author in care of Llewellyn Worldwide, and we will forward your request. Both the author and publisher appreciate hearing from you and learning of your enjoyment of this book and how it has helped you. Llewellyn Worldwide cannot guarantee that every letter written to the author can be answered, but all will be forwarded. Please write to:

Judith Page and Jan A. Malique
℅ Llewellyn Worldwide
2143 Wooddale Drive
Woodbury, MN 55125-2989

Please enclose a self-addressed stamped envelope for reply,
or $1.00 to cover costs. If outside the USA, enclose
an international postal reply coupon.

Many of Llewellyn's authors have websites with additional information and resources. For more information, please visit our website at http://www.llewellyn.com.

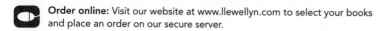

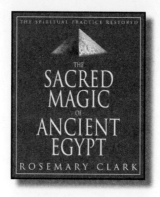

The Sacred Magic of Ancient Egypt
The Spiritual Practice Restored
ROSEMARY CLARK

For those who seek a deeper realization of Egypt's legacy, here is a guide to living the history of a culture that believed its sacred tradition was a timeless conduit to divine knowledge.

With an elaborate canon of religious and philosophical wisdom that is conveyed through hymns, litanies, spells, and ceremonies, *The Sacred Magic of Ancient Egypt* offers the serious practitioner an authentic blueprint for creating a modern temple and entering an exclusive dimension of the ancient mysteries.

978-1-56718-130-2, 416 pp., 7½ x 9⅛ $29.95

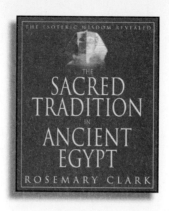

The Sacred Tradition in Ancient Egypt

The Esoteric Wisdom Revealed

ROSEMARY CLARK

Our modern quest for the wisdom of ancient Egypt centers on the true meaning of the symbolism, temples, tombs, and pyramids of this enigmatic motherland.

Egyptologist Rosemary Clark, who reads Egyptian hieroglyphics first-hand, examines the esoteric tradition of Egypt in remarkable detail. She explores dimensions of the language, cosmology, and temple life to show that a sacred mandate—the transformation of the human condition into its original cosmic substance—formed the foundation of Egypt's endeavors and still has great relevance today.

In addition, *The Sacred Tradition in Ancient Egypt* outlines the technology that utilized cyclic resonance, ritual, and sacred architecture to effect this ultimate stage in human evolution.

978-1-56718-129-6, 576 pp., 7½ x 9⅛ $29.95

The Inner Guide to Egypt

A Mystical Journey Through Time & Consciousness

ALAN RICHARDSON AND B. WALKER–JOHN

The Inner Guide to Egypt is both a tantalizing tour of Egyptian culture and a unique tool for spiritual enrichment, guiding you on a self-initiation into the Egyptian Mysteries. This rich system for spiritual development uses the Nile as a metaphor for astral travel. As you journey along this river of consciousness to visit sacred sites, you will discover how each site corresponds to physiological and psychological functions within. Guided meditations and visualization exercises enliven this ancient tradition, inviting you to explore shamanism; deities, gods, and goddesses; burial rites; hieroglyphics; the Great Pyramids; and Ka, the Egyptian concept of the soul.

978-0-7387-1875-0, 216 pp., 6 x 9 $17.95

Ancient Teachings for Beginners

Learn About Auras, Chakras, Angels & Astral Projection

DOUGLAS DE LONG

Uncover hidden knowledge from the mystery schools of ages past. This book is designed to awaken or enhance your psychic abilities in a very quick and profound manner. Rather than taking years to achieve this state, you will notice results within a few short weeks, if not instantly. Explore hidden secrets of the ancient mystery schools as you progress through each chapter, from opening your third eye and crown chakras to seeing and reading the human aura.

In addition, you will explore kundalini and chakra arousal techniques that are essential training for aura readers and future medical intuitives. Learn to safely work with spirit guides and angels, practice astral projection, and perform past-life recall.

978-1-56718-214-9, 264 pp., 5³⁄₁₆ x 8 $12.95

Ancient Healing Techniques

A Course in Psychic & Spiritual Development

DOUGLAS DE LONG

Learn to use ancient wisdom to become a powerful healing instrument. Thousands of years ago, the High Priests of Egypt performed a special rite called a Final Initiation. Many of these secret ceremonies took place at the Great Pyramid, where initiates performed sacred rituals involving breathing, meditating, and chanting. Afterwards, the students were ready to enter the world as healers.

The author of *Ancient Teachings for Beginners*, Douglas De Long, demonstrates how to perform this Final Initiation rite and other methods for advancing one's psychic and healing abilities. These techniques—involving energy healing, chakra work, colors, chanting, and breathing—are designed to help one achieve spiritual, emotional, and physical well-being.

978-0-7387-0650-4, 264 pp., 5³/₁₆ x 8   **$15.95**

Magical Pathworking

Techniques of Active Imagination

NICK FARRELL

Unlock the secrets of your mind and rule your Inner Kingdom!

Personality refinement is a precursor to serious spiritual work. Through techniques of pathworking (guided meditation), your imagination can shine a magic mirror on your personality. This inner landscape reveals your world as your unconscious sees it—a perspective that enables you to make dramatic changes, even to the point of rooting out neuroses and recovering from psychological trauma.

Become the ruler of your own Inner Kingdom with pathworking information that has been in the hands of the the Western Mystery schools for centuries. Nick Farrell unveils this secret material along with his own extensive research into imagination and mind magic.

978-0-7387-0407-4, 240 pp., 6 x 9   **$16.95**

To order, call 1-877-NEW-WRLD
Prices subject to change without notice
Order at Llewellyn.com 24 hours a day, 7 days a week!

Egyptian Paganism

Bring the Gods & Goddesses of Ancient Egypt into Daily Life

JOCELYN ALMOND AND KEITH SEDDON

Practice a modern form of Paganism based on an ancient Egyptian religion with *Egyptian Paganism*. People are turning to the ancient Egyptian deities in increasing numbers. Pagan organizations, especially the International Fellowship of Isis (with 20,000 members), have stimulated this growing interest. For solitary practitioners who want to perform daily devotions, this straightforward guide contains genuine invocations and prayers for each of the main deities, as well as a general overview of the deeper spiritual and magical aspects. There are translations of authentic religious texts along with practical instructions for creating a shrine, casting a circle, consecrating statues, and invoking deities.

978-0-7387-0438-8, 288 pp., 5³⁄₁₆ x 8   **$13.95**

Plant Spirit Journey

Discover the Healing Energies of the Natural World

LAURA SILVANA

Laura Silvana is a medical and spiritual intuitive whose mediumship abilities extend into the world of nature spirits. Born with an ability to see and hear spirits, her fascinating true story includes the wisdom imparted from a powerful shaman who taught her how to work with the energies of the plant kingdom.

Silvana tunes in to individual flowers and herbs and lets the plants speak for themselves. Dandelions possess a whimsical vibration to help counteract despair. Lilacs offer contentment and stability during times of transition. Red clover is a powerful healer that inspires courage, will, and determination.

This guide reveals the spiritual and emotional healing properties of thirty versatile plants and gives simple instructions for making plant spirit remedies at home. Both the plants and the ailments they treat are cross-referenced, so you can easily find the information you seek.

978-0-7387-1863-7, 288 pp., 6 x 9 $16.95